G.E.M. ANSCOMBE AND THE CATHOLIC INTELLECTUAL TRADITION

Published by the
NEUMANN UNIVERSITY PRESS

Neumann University
One Neumann Drive
Aston, Pennsylvania 19104-1298

http://www.neumann.edu/

Collection copyright © 2016 | ISBN 978-1-944769-12-3

G.E.M. ANSCOMBE AND THE CATHOLIC INTELLECTUAL TRADITION

Edited by John Mizzoni, Philip Pegan & Geoffrey Karabin

Table of Contents

Prologue: The Living Legacy of G.E.M. Anscombe 5
Gerard P. O'Sullivan

Part I   Introduction
1. G.E.M. Anscombe and the Catholic Intellectual Tradition . 11
   John Mizzoni, Philip Pegan, & Geoffrey Karabin
2. Recollections of Elizabeth Anscombe 17
   Joseph M. Boyle, Jr.

Part II   Anscombe and Catholic Moral Theory
3. G.E.M. Anscombe and Catholic Moral Thought 25
   Dennis J. Billy, C.Ss.R.
4. Clarifying Anscombe's Ethical Absolutism 49
   Justin Anderson

Part III   Anscombe and Double Effect
5. Intended and Unintended Consequences:
   A Natural Distinction? 83
   Jonathan Buttaci
6 The Ethical Relevance of the Intended/Foreseen
   Distinction According to Anscombe..........................117
   T.A. Cavanaugh

Part IV   Anscombe on Embryos, Souls, and Persons
7. Anscombe on Embryos and Persons............................ 143
   David Hershenov & Rose Hershenov
8. How Much Ontological Baggage
   Do Religious Practices Carry? Anscombe on Prayer
   to and for the Pre-resurrected Dead 161
   Peter Furlong & Michael Staron
9. Anscombe on the Immortality of the Soul 179
   Jeremy Bell

Editors and Contributors 195

Prologue
The Living Legacy
of G.E.M. Anscombe

Gerard P. O'Sullivan

The influence of Gertrude Elizabeth Margaret Anscombe and her husband Peter Geach on philosophical thought over the past seventy years cannot be overestimated. They reignited the moral imagination in philosophy and brought new life to a branch of thought which had degenerated into a mere cataloging of axioms. Anscombe's 1958 essay "Modern Moral Philosophy" restored the reputation of aretaic philosophy, or philosophical thinking about virtue, to contemporary discourse – and with no little thanks to Aristotle and Aquinas, to whom Anscombe owed a considerable debt.

To weigh the influence of Anscombe upon succeeding generations without, and at the very same time considering the significance of her Catholicism would be foolhardy, as several of the papers in this remarkable collection demonstrate. Anscombe was converted to Catholicism during a time when British intellectuals were discovering or rediscovering the Church in droves.

G. K. Chesterton, whose books first led Anscombe to Rome, was a relative latecomer to Catholicism. He waited until 1922, at the surprisingly ripe age of forty-eight, before joining the *confirmandi*. Chesterton had been defending the Roman Catholic Church for years but as something of a bystander, clinging tenaciously to Anglo-Catholicism until late middle age. And on the occasion of his full acceptance into the Church his waggish friend George Bernard Shaw wrote, "Gilbert, this is going too far."

Anscombe, like Chesterton and many other intellectuals of their generation, gravitated to Roman Catholicism as the sanctuary of wisdom that it is – and especially in the years between the wars, when Europe found itself in a shambles after Armistice. Few historians of that period remember the power exerted upon post-war Catholic Britain by Spode House, a conference center maintained by the Dominicans of Blackfriars and overseen, for much of its intensely rich history, by Father Conrad Pepler, OP.

Father Conrad, as he was known to all, was founding Warden of the first Roman Catholic conference center in the United Kingdom. He was also the priest made unintentionally famous when he conferred conditional absolution on a dying Ludwig Wittgenstein in 1951. Fr. Conrad recited the office while surrounded by the philosopher's kneeling friends – among them Wittgenstein's protégé Elizabeth Anscombe.

Anscombe and her husband Peter Geach met at Blackfriars on the Feast of Corpus Christi in 1938. They, like so many Oxford and Cambridge intellectuals, were drawn to Blackfriars and Spode House, the latter of which was maintained by Fr. Conrad and his Dominican brothers as a site dedicated to what Augustine called "the tranquility of order." In the years between the wars and after, this phrase guided Spode House and the community of Catholic and non-Catholic intellectuals which gathered within its walls.

Groups of men and women assembled in this quiet, convivial Staffordshire setting to debate the finer points of Thomism and attempt to reassemble the pieces of a culture left in ruins. It was here that Anscombe and Geach previewed some of their most insightful papers, surrounded by others steeped in the classical and contemporary philosophical traditions. Spode House was, for all intents and purposes, the birthplace of what we today call "analytical Thomism" and the place beyond Oxford where Wittgenstein could converse most openly with his Dominican students – Frs. Herbert McCabe, Conrad Pepler, Cornelius Ernst, and Fergus Kerr among them.

For Anscombe and Geach, Catholicism was something which they lived and breathed every day of their rich married lives together. It brought them into contact with Spode House and made them an integral part of the Catholic ferment of modern European life. Ergo, their immersion in analytical philosophy and Thomism was not merely something they thought about. It was something they did. And this cannot be unbundled and unwound from their faith.

This wonderful volume of papers owes a great debt of thanks to Drs. John Mizzoni, Philip Pegan and Geoffrey Karabin of the Neumann University philosophy faculty. Together Professors Mizzoni, Pegan and Karabin inaugurated the annual Anscombe Forum as homage to the memory of G.E.M. Anscombe on the event of her 95th birthday in 2014.

Every year, in March, thinkers who are working within the living tradition of Anscombe and Geach gather on Neumann's campus in Aston, Pennsylvania and bring to life again that great convivium that was Spode House in its heyday. And every year hereafter may the participants gather together and raise their glasses high in toast to the lives and legacies of two of Catholicism and the west's most distinguished thinkers.

Part 1
Introduction

1. G.E.M. Anscombe and the Catholic Intellectual Tradition

John Mizzoni, Philip Pegan & Geoffrey Karabin

The papers in this volume are drawn from a conference held on March 14-15, 2014 at Neumann University, in Aston, Pennsylvania. Neumann University is a small, Catholic Franciscan university located in the greater Philadelphia area. We are grateful to everyone who helped to make Neumann's inaugural conference on the thought of Anscombe such a wonderful success. We thank the presenters, the chairs of the sessions, the staff of Neumann University, as well as Gerard O'Sullivan, formerly the Vice President for Academic Affairs at Neumann, who provided support and encouragement throughout the planning and hosting of the conference.

March 2014 marked the 95th birthday of G.E.M. Anscombe (1919 – 2001), one of the twentieth century's most provocative and highly regarded philosophers, who was also a pupil of Ludwig Wittgenstein. Anscombe is known for challenging received philosophical views, and some commentators have regarded her as the greatest woman philosopher of all time.

Many conferences on Anscombe's work have focused on her contributions to moral philosophy, virtue ethics, and action theory. The conference held at Neumann focused on the question: What are Anscombe's contributions—actual and potential—to the Catholic intellectual tradition? Conference participants worked with this question through an exploration of a wide range of themes from Anscombe's work, including contraception, personhood, the soul, the will, marriage, and the doctrine of double effect, among other topics. Some papers explored how her Catholic faith influenced her approach to philosophy and how her faith influenced the types of philosophical issues with which she dealt. The present volume contains a selection of these papers. The volume unfortunately does not contain Candace Vogler's talk "Anscombe's Complaint: The Importance of Moral Prohibition," as it had been previously promised to another publisher. As a continuation of the first, introductory, part of this book, the second essay, written by Joseph Boyle, recounts his and his family's experiences in knowing Elizabeth Anscombe, as an astute, forceful, and courageous Catholic philosopher. Yet Boyle goes beyond offering an account of Anscombe the philosopher; he provides insight into Elizabeth Anscombe as a good friend. What is particularly notable about Boyle's account is Anscombe' authenticity, not only with regard to her pursuit of truth, but in terms of living out those truths in concrete relationships.

In the second part of the volume, the authors focus on Anscombe's contributions to Catholic moral theory. First, Fr. Dennis Billy gives an overview of Anscombe as a Catholic philosopher and reviews some of Anscombe's work in moral theory, as it bears on and has influenced Catholic moral theory. He also discusses how Catholic thought was influential on Anscombe herself. In the next paper, Justin Anderson seeks to clarify Anscombe's ethical absolutism, which is an important dimension of Catholic ethics. Anderson proposes to do this by tying her commitment to ethical absolutism to her work on intention. According to Anderson, Anscombe seeks to articulate an account of ethics whose foundation, while focused on intentional action, is not reduced to a purely subjective or internal mental state. In this account, ethics must be understood both in terms of what the agent thinks as well as what the agent does. Anderson points out how Anscombe's work on this theme is relevant to contemporary Thomism, along with the nature of ethical absolutism, an ethical absolutism, Anderson argues, which is misunderstood by some prominent contemporary Anscombean scholars.

Part three of the volume contains two papers focusing on Anscombe's work on double effect or, 'side effects,' as she preferred to call it (see the enclosed papers by Billy, Buttaci, and Cavanaugh). As with ethical absolutism, the principle of double effect has occupied an important place in Catholic ethics; specifically, as a means for analyzing the morality of good actions that become entangled in evil. Just as Anderson in part II sought to reconcile themes from Anscombe's earlier and later works, in part III Jonathan Buttaci— with a series of clever examples—attempts to clarify how Anscombe can consistently allow that there are "external constraints on the content of our intentions." This is a position, says Buttaci, which may not initially appear Anscombean if we only consider her earlier work. In brief, the idea is that 'the ordinary course of things' plays a role in determining under which descriptions an act is intentional. This idea, Buttaci argues, can be used to support Anscombe's judgments about some famous cases. Buttaci draws upon Aristotelian metaphysics to enrich and support the view he defends.

In the sixth paper of the volume T.A. Cavanaugh lays out the moral importance of the intended/foreseen distinction that Anscombe defends (a distinction essential for the principle of double effect). He argues that the intended/foreseen distinction is important, not only for resisting the lure of consequentialism, but also because it is crucial to any ethics, such as Catholic ethics, that recognizes absolute prohibitions, the intrinsic badness of certain acts, and the importance of virtue and vice. In the final section of his paper Cavanaugh notes that the intended/foreseen distinction is part of moral psychology and credits Anscombe with doing much to show, and remind us, that "moral psychology is morally important psychology."

Part four of the volume brings together three papers that examine some of Anscombe's work on embryos, souls, and persons. David and Rose Hershenov open the section with an examination of Anscombe's arguments regarding the metaphysical and ethical status of embryos. They show that Anscombe provided "philosophical support [for] the Church's mandate that we treat embryos as one of us" even as she maintained that the early embryo was not a human being. They argue that "[t]here are many things to appreciate about Anscombe's position." Still, they argue, a better position is available. While Anscombe enlists Aquinas and facts about monozygotic twinning in support of her view that the early embryo is not a human being, the Hershenovs deploy Thomistic metaphysics and facts about twinning to support the view that a human being – or, in the case of monozygotic twins, two human beings – is (are) present from the moment of conception.

In essay eight Peter Furlong and Michael Staron focus their attention on Anscombe's claims about the human person after death in "The Immortality of the Soul," an early paper of hers that she did not publish. For Anscombe, puzzles arise when we consider the religious practice of praying to and for these deceased persons. What are these souls? Where are they? And are they immaterial substances? Anscombe is not satisfied with the concept 'immaterial substance'. And, according to Furlong and Staron, Anscombe was ultimately unable to specify a way to characterize the deceased in such a way that would make it intelligible for Catholics to pray to and for these persons.

Jeremy Bell, in essay nine, continues the analysis of Anscombe's paper on the immortality of the soul. The essay is a nuanced reflection on whether it is sensible to speak of immaterial substances. The gateway to that reflection is the question of whether one can sensibly talk about the immortality of a soul in a state between death and a resurrected body. Bell incorporates both the metaphysics of Aristotle and Thomas and argues, contra Anscombe, that it is possible, at least in principle, to sensibly call something an immaterial substance. Bell's work thereby contributes to a philosophical discussion of substance as well as provides a critique of Anscombe's understanding of substance.

Bell's critique, however, is far from dismissive. He sees Anscombe as involved in a philosophically heroic, but ultimately untenable project. Bell reasons that the difficulties that Anscombe encounters with this topic reveal "a deep tension between Anscombe's Wittgensteinianism and her Catholicism." Bell acknowledges that Anscombe has made real contributions to the Catholic intellectual tradition, but he suggests that "this contribution has lasting value perhaps *despite* Wittgenstein's influence, not because of it." Anscombe's commitment both to Catholic orthodoxy and the insights of Wittgenstein lead her, Bell concludes, to defend the belief in the existence of a soul that nonetheless cannot be identified with an entity.

Ultimately, all of the contributors to this volume are in agreement that Anscombe has indeed made a lasting impact not only on philosophy and ethics, but also on the Catholic intellectual tradition, broadly construed. In the context of discussing Anscombe's work on ethics, Cavanaugh said it best when he stated that we "need her profound insights," and "[d] eeply in her debt we remain."

2. Recollections of Elizabeth Anscombe

Joseph M. Boyle, Jr.

Many North American philosophers of my age cohort, completing degrees and getting first jobs around 1970, would have encountered Elizabeth Anscombe. Some might have studied with her, and some surely came to know her and her work better than I. But my wife, Barbara, and I were very fortunate to have gotten to know Professor Anscombe fairly well from the early 1980s until the early 1990s. We saw her once after that, at a meeting in Cambridge in 1997.

We first met Prof. Anscombe at the College of St. Thomas in Minnesota around 1980, where she gave a lecture. I became acquainted with her philosophically around this time at one or more Fellowship of Catholic Scholars' annual meetings. We had a memorable visit at our home in Houston in the spring of 1982, when she met our four children and engaged in conversation with each of them. Prof. Anscombe was in Houston for the American Catholic Philosophical Association annual meeting at which she was awarded the

Association's Aquinas Medal, and where she presented her important paper on "Action, Intention and 'Double Effect.'"

Barbara and I got to know her better during a wonderful week in Rome in the Spring of 1986 at a conference on Catholic ethical issues—where she savaged a paper of mine dealing with the culpability required for grave sin (and seemed slightly abashed when, after the session, she was surrounded by a group of elderly clerical moralists, who said, in effect, that her refutation was not traditional). That is the meeting where Prof. Anscombe presented her provocative list of 20 opinions of Anglo-American philosophers which she believed incompatible with Christian faith. We were put up in the same hotel as Prof. Anscombe, and we enjoyed many meals and sightseeing outings, as well as a memorable visit to the Vatican that included an audience with Pope St. John Paul II.

After we moved to Toronto she stopped there a number of times en route to Minnesota for family visits, and stayed with us twice. These proved to be memorable events in our family's history.

As many of you know, there exists a treasure trove of usually hilarious Anscombe and Anscombe/Geach anecdotes. Her unconventional personality and philosophical greatness guarantee this. I suspect I have contributed a little to that treasure trove, and could do so again here, but let me instead settle for a few general reflections about this great Catholic philosopher.

I have met a number of people who have found Elizabeth Anscombe's abrupt and intense style of interacting to be off-putting and rude. Several professional friends found her simply unacceptable. Her critique of C.S. Lewis' discussion of naturalism in *Miracles*, thought by many to have been savage, is perhaps the best-known example of this aspect of her personality.[1] I have been on the wrong end of her philosophical criticisms enough times to know what people are talking about.

But Barbara's and my overwhelming experience in interacting with an older Elizabeth Anscombe was delight and edification in the company of an admittedly unconventional and intense, but endlessly curious and lively friend, who was full of fun and very happy to take it at her own expense. Of all the philosophers who visited our home over the decades, few made any favorable impact whatsoever on our four children— 'another one of dad's friends;' yet Elizabeth engaged each of them in focused conversation and all fondly remember her and their conversations with her.

Of course, Professor Anscombe took philosophical questions very seriously and engaged them with a rare intensity. She was at least as formidable in the flesh as her writings suggest, and often would not suffer fools gladly.

One aspect of her commitment to philosophy was that she was ready to think through—argue through from the beginning—any philosophical topic that arose, however definitively she had addressed the matter previously. I think that Professor Anscombe did not regard any philosophical issue as simply settled and put to bed, but was ready to go at it

---

[1] Anscombe made reference to this event in the introduction to *Metaphysics and the Philosophy of Mind: Collected Papers, Volume II* (Minneapolis: University of Minnesota Press, 1981), ix-x. She did not believe that Lewis found the event a 'horrible and shocking experience' as some friends reported, and she expressed admiration for the revision of his argument by Lewis. Anscombe made many of the points in these pages to me in conversation, emphasizing a difference in Lewis's response to her and that of his friends, and her respect for his efforts to revise the argument. Professor Anscombe presented a paper on this matter to the Oxford C.S. Lewis Society in the early 1980s, and this, or a reconstruction of it from notes and a recording, will likely be published. I thank Luke Gormally for reminding me of the introduction to Volume II, and the information about this as yet unpublished talk.

again, just for the fun of it, and maybe because something new might come to light. So if you like philosophy, and don't mind getting beat up a bit, or maybe even more than a bit, Elizabeth was really fun to be with.

During the days she stayed with us, she would shop with Barbara more or less all day, and then argue with me about such things as voluntariness, lying, and what St. Thomas had to say about these things, LONG into the night. I distinctly remember the end of one of these visits: she took along in the car my copy of the *Prima Secundae*[2] as we drove Elizabeth to Pearson Airport, to get in an extra half hour of interpretation and argument.

This passion for philosophy never left her. When we last saw her in 1997, she was obviously frail and not fully herself. She attended all the sessions at the four-day conference on Catholic bioethics sponsored by the Linacre Centre (now the Anscombe Centre) at Cambridge University. She intervened as usual and enjoyed herself thoroughly—making fun of her infirmities. I gave a paper on cooperation with evil and the issue of a continental practice of counseling those who were considering abortion arose. Part of this protocol was that the counselor was to sign a form saying that the person seeking abortion had been counseled; that signed form was required to proceed. I argued that the cooperation of the counselor was material cooperation only, but that it might nevertheless be impermissible. Afterwards she said to me, in what I believe was our last conversation, something very like: "Joe, there is only one thing they can do with that signed form." I said: "that does not make it formal cooperation." She responded, a little put out: "I did not say that it was formal cooperation. I said there is only one thing they can do with it."

---

[2] This is the part of St. Thomas Aquinas's *Summa Theologiae* dealing with ethical theory.

Another aspect of Professor Anscombe's unconventional and intense way of being was her utter fearlessness. This was especially evident when important moral or religious matters were at stake, and when others' moral perceptions were clouded by bad theory or political concerns. Two of her papers on war especially exhibit this fearlessness. Her undergraduate pamphlet, questioning the justice of England's war effort in the fall of 1939 shows courage and moral clarity that is not evident, for example, in the Vatican's statements at the time. She rightly worried that England was committed, or would be, to the kind of strategic bombing of cities later to be condemned by Vatican II, and most of humanity. In this she was prophetic; saying England's war was unjust in the fall of 1939 took courage, especially for an undergraduate.

The moral judgment underlying her other famous pamphlet, on Mr. Truman's Degree is still unaccepted by many Americans, including some Catholic scholars, but her judgment seems to me undeniable on pro-life or just war grounds. Bombing those cities was wrong. Many of Anscombe's colleagues at the time agreed, but not many showed up for the Oxford convocation vote on the matter. Only Philippa Foot, her colleague at Summerville College, Foot's husband M. R. D. Foot, and another philosopher voted with her.[3] The relevant correspondence I saw from Professor Anscombe's papers make very interesting reading; some letters were congratulatory letters of support but several contained arguments against Anscombe's condemnation, on the grounds that the bombs saved lives. There is also a follow up letter from the woman in Zeeland, who was quoted in the pamphlet as complaining – with reason Anscombe acknowledged – about allied bombing of the dykes in Zeeland late in World War II.

---

[3]Luke Gormally provided this detail, and corrections about my recollections of the correspondence in Anscombe's paper, in an email comment on a draft of this paper.

Professor Anscombe's pro-life protest, recorded by a newspaper photograph of her being dragged away by the police; her blunt defense of the received Catholic teaching on contraception; her dismissive treatment of the whole movement of Oxford style moral reflection as rather provincial in ignoring Christianity's insistence on moral absolutes – all these show a person who when faced with the opinions of others that contradict her own reasoned judgments, especially if her judgments were closely connected to her Catholic faith, would maintain the truth as she understood it and affirm it in the most effective way she could, whatever others thought of her.

Part 2

Anscombe and Catholic Moral Theory

3. G. E. M. Anscombe and Catholic Moral Thought

Dennis J. Billy, C.Ss.R.

My purpose in this paper is to cover in broad strokes the impact of Anscombe's thought on the Catholic intellectual tradition and, more specifically, on the discipline of Catholic moral thought, both philosophical and theological. With these strokes I hope to paint a general portrait of Anscombe as a Catholic philosopher and her contribution to Catholic moral thought, while leaving the more difficult task of assessing the particulars of her various moral arguments to others in this conference more skilled in this area than I.

Before doing so, however, I think it would first be necessary to say something about the impact the Catholic intellectual tradition had on her. It is also important to mention at the very outset that, by "Catholic intellectual tradition," I do not wish to imply that Catholic thought is confined to a single philosophical or theological approach or fail to acknowledge that the Catholic faith actually encompasses a variety of intellectual and spiritual traditions that have been a source of enrichment to the Church's faith (e.g., Pauline, Augustinian, Thomistic thought—to name but a few). To do so, would be to greatly misunderstand the Church's universal calling to be "all things to all" and to "make disciples of all nations" (1Cor 9:22; Mt 28:19).

Nor do I wish to confuse it with Sacred Tradition, which along with Sacred Scripture constitutes a single deposit of the Word of God entrusted to the Church and interpreted by its living magisterium (Second Vatican Council, 1965[1], nos. 7-10). By "Catholic intellectual tradition," I am simply referring to those philosophical, theological, and spiritual modes of thought that have weathered the test of time and been found helpful in both the development, expression, and enculturation of Catholic orthodoxy at various points in history. If "[t]radition," as Jaroslav Pelikan tells us, "is the living faith of the dead," not "the dead faith of the living," (Pelikan, 1984, p. 65) then Anscombe, I believe, was someone whose thought was informed by the living faith of the Catholic Church and who sought to make that faith even more alive by living out her convictions and following them wherever they led her.

G. E. M. Anscombe (1919-2001): Intentional Catholic

Almost an exact contemporary of the late Pope John Paul II (1920-2005), Anscombe would be the first to point out that Catholic thought had an enormous influence on her own life. During her secondary school years, she was known to have been an avid reader of theological works and was particularly influenced by the writings of G.K. Chesterton. In fact, she is at times referred to as a member of the "Chesterton generation," that group of twentieth-century Catholic intellectuals who were influenced by writings of the great "prince of paradox" and which one commentator says exuded "a confidence and a 'joy and peace in believing'"(Daly, 1994, p. viii). Her curiosity about matters of faith and her spiritual and intellectual dissatisfaction with Anglicanism led to inquiries with the Dominicans of Blackfriars College, Oxford, who facilitated her conversion to Catholicism in 1938. It was at Blackfriars College, moreover, where she met Peter Geach, a fellow philosopher and convert to Catholicism, whom she married in 1941 and with whom she raised a family of seven children. It is also significant that she collaborated on a number of occasions with her husband, whose specialty was logic and the history of philosophy and who was an influential figure in what later came to be known as Analytical Thomism (Vincelette, 2011, p. 184; Gormally, 1994, pp. 1-5).[1]

At a time when much attention is given to the formation of "intentional disciples" (Weddell, 2012, pp. 64-67), it is important to note that Anscombe, who wrote what is arguably the most important work on human intention of the twentieth century (Anscombe, 1957), was for all practical purposes what we might call an "intentional Catholic." By this I mean, her conversion to the Catholic faith, her vocation to the lay state, specifically to married and family life, and her profession as a philosopher, were deeply intertwined with her love for truth and her impassioned embrace of Catholic orthodoxy. This was an intellectual and spiritual outlook on life that touched her deeply, shaped her convictions about the nature of truth, and to which she was intensely loyal. It gave her a unique vantage point from which to survey the philosophical problems of her day and served as the backdrop against which she lived out her vocation and conducted her philosophical research. It also propelled her to live out her moral convictions in the public square even when they ran against the tide of public

---

[1] For an example of this collaborative effort, see Anscombe and Geach, (1961). For a complete Anscombe bibliography, see Gormally, Kietzmann, and Torralba (2012).

opinion and got her into trouble with legal authorities, as in the case of her arrests for anti-abortion protests in the 1970s.

Like many other well-known converts—John Henry Newman, G.K. Chesterton, Frederick Copleston, Ronald Knox, Jacques Maritain, Edith Stein, Dietrich von Hildebrand, Avery Dulles, and Alasdair MacIntyre (to name but a few)— Anscombe's journey to Catholicism involved a carefully reasoned search for truth which brought her to belief in Jesus Christ as the Son of God and Redeemer of the human race. It also involved a journey of the mind that led to a deep understanding and conviction that the Catholic Church was established by Christ to safeguard the deposit of faith and promulgate the Gospel message throughout history. As a philosopher, she understood the limitations of human reason and did her best to ensure that its conclusions were well argued, based on solid evidence, and to the point. She had little patience with poor, hastily constructed arguments (whether for or against the faith) and took them apart with precise reasoning that both went to the core of the problem and pointed the way to a possible resolution. Her famous debate with C.S. Lewis at the Oxford Socratic Club in 1948 about his assertion in the book *Miracles* (1947) that "Naturalism" is self-refuting is a case in point, as was her active and lively participation in Catholic philosophical discussions at the Spode House Conference Center, Straffordshire from 1942-1972 (Anscombe, 1981[7]; McGrath, 2013, pp. 250-59; Vincelette, 2011, p. 184).

Moreover, we cannot speak of the influence of the Catholic intellectual tradition on Anscombe without adverting at some point to her understanding of her role in the Church's life and mission. The body is one but has many members (1Cor 12:12). God's grace flows from Christ to the members of his body in a variety of ways to provide for the needs of the Church, perfect her, and highlight her dignity and beauty.[2] The theology of the various states of life within the Church—priestly, religious, and lay—forms a part of this rich tradition, and we would be remiss to think that Anscombe was unaware of its general contours and how it impacted her life within the Church and her profession as a Catholic philosopher. Indeed, it goes without saying that, as an intentional convert to Catholicism who took her faith seriously, she saw her primary responsibility before God as working out her salvation as a married Catholic lay woman by participating in the sacramental life of the Church, being faithful in her married and family life, and bringing the Gospel into the marketplace of the temporal sphere of life. She understood that the specific role of the laity was "to make the Church present and fruitful in those places and circumstances where only through them can it become the salt of the earth" (Second Vatican Council, 1964, no. 33).[3]

Anscombe lived out her Catholic Christian life, first and foremost, through her marriage to Peter Geach and her dedication to her family. These concerns were central to her life and impacted her intellectual life in many ways, both large and small. Luke Gormally, her son-in-law and the editor of a *Festschrift* dedicated to the couple on the occasion of their fiftieth wedding anniversary, says "...the commitment of each to serious work in philosophy has been sustained by the Christian faith which has informed their life together as husband and wife; for the demands of marriage when taken seriously both test and deepen Christian faith. And a deepened Christian faith," he adds, "in the sensitivity it nourishes to the

---

[2] For a treatment of the different duties or states within the Church, one which Anscombe would have known and recognized, see Thomas Aquinas, *Summa theologiae*, II-II, q. 183, a. 2.

[3] For an expanded treatment of the vocation of the laity, see John Paul II, 1988, nos. 1-64; *Catechism of the Catholic Church*, nos. 897-913. All of these works appeared during Anscombe's lifetime; *Lumen Gentium*, a key Vatican II document, came out when she was at the height of her career.

claims of truth, preserves one from the kind of philosophizing which, whatever its ingenuity, amounts to little more than a rationalizing defense of the naturalistic assumptions of our disintegrating culture" (Gormally, 1994, p. 3). In the same volume, Cardinal Cahal B. Daly points to "their fifty years of philosophical, spiritual, and personal married partnership" and says "…they have given us a model of personal faith and Christian witness and of sacramentally hallowed and faith-deepened partnership in Christian marriage, which are the source of inspiration to all" (Daly, 1994, ix). This tribute points to how the couple's married life informed their profession as Catholic philosophers and inspired them to use their God-given talents to make the Church present in the marketplace of ideas, especially in the field of philosophical inquiry to which they were each so deeply dedicated.

But let us not overly idealize our portrayal of Anscombe. As a person, she had her own unique character quirks and idiosyncrasies that readily revealed the jagged contours of her personality and her sometimes humorous (even laughable) human foibles. According to one commentator, "…the large-statured and fierce-in-debate Anscombe received the moniker 'Dragon Lady' and was known to sport a monocle, to smoke cigars… to swear like a sailor… and unless you were the pope to refuse to wear a dress as opposed to her normal attire of pants" (Vincelette, 2011, p. 184). Other sources attest to these and other personal eccentricities. *The Telegraph* writes that "[c]lad in leopard-skin trousers and a leather jacket she might sit in silence for minutes on end, puffing on a cigar, after one of her students had finished reading out an essay" (Oppenheimer, 2011). *The Guardian* tells us that "[f]or a time she sported a monocle and had a trick of raising her eyebrows and letting it fall on her ample bosom, which somehow made her yet more daunting" (Oppenheimer, 2011). Another commentator observes: "In 1968 when much of the rest of the Catholic intellectual world reacted with shock and anger to Pope Paul VI's reaffirmation of Catholic teaching regarding the immorality of contraception, the Geach-Anscombe family toasted the announcement with champagne" (George, 2001). Bold, fearless, even shocking, gestures such as these were a reflection of Anscombe's mind. At Oxford, where she taught philosophy for over twenty years, and later at Cambridge, she was an eccentric, indomitable personality not to be ignored and whose arguments had to be reckoned with lest they come back to unsettle, disturb, and even haunt. Her manner of doing philosophy was straightforward, confident, and uniquely her own. Her writing style was "dense and unrepetitive," making it "hard to know sometimes whether it would be more clarificatory to go on to the next sentence, or to return to the previous one" (Geach, 2005, p. xiii). She loved to argue and, as her daughter, philosopher Mary Geach, states, "was always ready for a bout" (Geach, 2005, p. xxi). "Philosophy as she does it is fresh," another commentator notes, "her arguments take unexpected turns and make unexpected connections, and show always how much there is that had not been seen before" (Dolan, 2001).

G. E. M. Anscombe: Catholic Philosopher

A disciple of Ludwig Wittgenstein who succeeded him in his chair at Cambridge and who as his translator and one of his literary executors was probably most responsible for making him known in the English-speaking world, Anscombe was also a serious and devout convert to the Catholic faith. She was not a philosopher who simply happened to be a Catholic and whose faith had little (if anything) to do with her program of philosophical inquiry. On the contrary, her faith informed her reasoned search for truth, while at the same time enabling her to remain true to the strictest standards of her profession. She herself saw no contradiction between her Catholic faith and analytic philosophy's careful examination of language as a preferred method for doing philosophy. "Analytical philosophy," she says, "is more characterized by styles of argument and investigation than by doctrinal content. It is thus possible for people of widely different beliefs to be practitioners of this sort of philosophy. It ought not to surprise anyone that a seriously believing Catholic Christian should also be an analytical philosopher" (Anscombe, 2008, p. 66). Analytical philosophy, we might say, provided Anscombe with a method for distinguishing truth from falsehood and goodness from badness. It was not the only instrument in her philosopher's bag of tools, but it was a powerful one, and one she was exceedingly good at using. She employed this analytical method in the service of her faith by taking on many controversial issues that were important to her Catholic faith and that demanded a clear-eyed, reasoned analysis in the service of the truth. Rather than being a hindrance to her philosophical endeavors, her Catholicism actually gave her a unique vantage point from which to view the issues at hand, see them in perspective, and identify angles that many of her contemporaries either overlooked or simply could not see.

In his encyclical, *Fides et Ratio*, John Paul II identifies three stances of philosophy toward theology. The first employs a philosophical approach completely outside of faith and the deposit of revelation; the second seeks to develop a specifically Christian philosophy; the third places philosophy in the service of theology. The Pope recognizes the strengths and weaknesses of each approach. The first must deal with the inherent weakness of human reason, yet benefits from philosophy's aspiration to seek the truth in the natural order and remains open—at least implicitly—to the supernatural. The second seeks to find a genuinely Christian way of philosophizing, recognizing all the while that the Church has never adopted an official philosophy. The third has theology calling upon philosophy to help it clarify the deposit of faith and the truths of revelation (John Paul II, 1998, nos.

75-77; Morris, 2010, pp. 192-93). A look at Anscombe's philosophical writings indicates that she worked primarily in the first stance (e.g., Anscombe, 1957) and ventured at times into the second (e.g., Anscombe, 1972; Anscombe, 1981[4]) and third (e.g., Anscombe, 1981[1]; Anscombe, 1981[6]). Even when she was working from the first stance, however, where she philosophized outside of the context of faith and revelation, it is clear that she never checked her faith at the threshold of reason's inner sanctum, but used it to challenge reason to shed its sometimes narrow and restrictive ways of viewing reality and to call forth its deepest potential. In this respect, she appropriated from her faith certain rationally based insights that enabled her to carry out her task of philosophizing in an even more profound and penetrating manner.

Anscombe, in this respect, was a philosopher's philosopher. For her, this discipline involved simply "thinking about the most difficult and ultimate questions" (Geach, 2005, p. xiii).[4] She anticipated John Paul II's challenge in *Fides et Ratio* "to trust in the power of human reason and not to set themselves goals that are too modest in their philosophizing" (John Paul II, 1998, no. 56). She also recognized, as John Paul himself asserts, that "[p]hilosophical thought is often the only ground for understanding and dialogue with those who do not share our faith" (John Paul II, 1998, no. 104). She did, in other words, what she knew how to do best: philosophize! She did not see any contradiction between her Catholic faith and her analytical approach to philosophy, but considered them as mutually enriching. These words of John F. Morris on the vocation of the Catholic philosopher resonate well with her philosophical vocation and intellectual corpus:

> In the end, the Church asks much of Catholic philosophers, both as "philosophers" and as "Catholics." This is because,

---

[4]According to her daughter, Mary Geach, this was the way Anscombe defined philosophy in her Cambridge university prospectus.

within the Catholic Tradition, philosophy is not merely
an esoteric sideline, but rather it is an integral part of the
work of the Church in breaking open the Wisdom of God
for both believers and non-believers alike. Nor must we
forget that, in doing this work, the Church does not ask
the Catholic philosopher to become a theologian. *Fides
et Ratio* tells us that the Church needs both theology
and philosophy. Now, some Catholic philosophers will
make a much closer use of theology in their efforts than
others, and such approaches are perfectly legitimate.
But equally important are Catholic philosophers whose
work is much less explicitly religious. All such efforts
are needed in metaphysics, natural theology, philosophy
of mind, bioethics, aesthetics, philosophy of the human
person, and so on. Catholic philosophers need to be
supportive of each other in all these various works, even
ones that fall outside of our own particular preferences
for how philosophy ought to be done in general, and
more specifically as members of the Catholic Church.
(Morris, 2010, p. 200)

Anscombe used her skills as an analytical philosopher to seek
the truth about some of the most basic (and controversial)
issues of her day—the purpose of modern moral philosophy,
the role of intention in the moral act, the existence of
exceptionless moral prohibitions, the proper use of the
principle of double effect, the dignity of the human being,
the spirituality of man, the role of the state, the use of
contraception, abortion, euthanasia, the just war— to name
but a few. In examining these issues, she sought the truth of
the matter at hand and, in serving the truth, believed she was
breaking open the Wisdom of God and thus participating in
the mission of the Church. The fact that she sought to do so
within a philosophical discipline that, unlike Neoplatonism,
or Thomism, or even Kantianism or Phenomenology (for

that matter), had few Catholic adherents and even fewer who sought to integrate its insights with those of the faith, indicates that she was true to her lay vocation of bringing the Gospel to the marketplace, which in terms of her profession, has to do with the marketplace of philosophical ideas.

Anscombe and Catholic Moral Theology

We are almost in a position to discuss Anscombe's impact on Catholic intellectual life and especially that of Catholic moral theology. For this to happen, however, it will first be necessary to understand that a philosopher can impact a theological tradition in different ways. He or she can have a direct and immediate influence as in the third stance of philosophy toward theology, when theology specifically calls upon philosophy to help it elucidate Catholic doctrine for a changing intellectual landscape. To cite just two examples, such was the case in late antiquity with Augustine in his adaptation of the Neoplatonism of Plotinus and in the High Middle Ages with Aquinas's use of Aristotle for their theological purposes. In these instances, each calls upon a particular philosophical tradition to help him further his goal of achieving a comprehensive synthesis of Christian theology (Pinckaers, 1995, pp. 195-239; Porter, 2013, pp. 70-91).

A philosopher, however, can also impact a theological tradition in a more indirect and mediate way, as when he or she helps bring about a paradigmatic shift in the culture and society of the times which, in turn, influences the way theologians frame the questions they ask and seek to resolve them methodologically. For example, such was the case with the way William of Ockham's Nominalism contributed to the dissolution of the Medieval synthesis (the so-called *via antiqua*), helped give rise to the modern era (the so-called *via moderna*), and influenced theologians by causing them to focus on the primacy of the will, particulars, and empirical observation. When applied to the history of moral theology (or perhaps it would be better to say the history of "Catholic moral thought," since moral theology did not exist as a separate theological discipline until after the Council of Trent and the rise of the Catholic seminary system), we see a general hermeneutical shift in moral discourse from the rhetorical and allegorical (as in Augustine's Neoplatonic synthesis of theology in late antiquity) to the dialectical (as in Aquinas's Aristotelian synthesis of theology in the thirteenth century) to the casuistic (as in the system of moral reasoning that developed after Ockham and the dissolution of the medieval synthesis and which arose during the period early modernity and continued in Catholic circles pretty much up to the dawn of the Second Vatican Council) (Pinckaers, 1995, pp. 240-79; Gilson, 1985, pp. 498- 99; Leff, 1976, pp. 1-31).[5]

In my judgment, Anscombe had both a direct and indirect influence on the development of Catholic moral thinking in the post-Vatican II era. To see this, it is important that we remember, in the first place, that there is often a lag in time between the appearance of a philosophical insight on the intellectual scene and when it is actually recognized and then utilized by moral theologians in their work. Since Anscombe's major ethical works appeared in 1957 (*Intention*) and 1958 ("Modern Moral Philosophy"), we should not expect her insights to have made their way into Catholic moral discourse for some time (let us say, until the end of the Council in 1965 and afterwards). In the second place, while it is true that the Catholic Church has no "official philosophy" (John Paul II, 1998, no. 10), it is also true that the philosophical thought of Thomas Aquinas has had a major impact in the direction and shape of Catholic moral thought and that it has, for all practical purposes, functioned in the past (truncated

---

[5]For the subsequent decline of virtue ethics in Western thought, see Frede (2013).

and narrowly interpreted as it may have been at times in the various historical forms of Thomism) as a kind of "unofficial philosophy." For these reasons, Anscombe's impact on Catholic moral theology was not immediate but delayed in time and largely overshadowed by more established philosophical voices within the tradition.

Moreover, as we evaluate Anscombe's impact on the Catholic intellectual life, we should also bear in mind Vatican II's call for a better understanding of the contemporary mind by relying "on a philosophical patrimony which is perennially valid and taking into account the philosophical investigations of later ages. This is especially true," it continues, "of those investigations which exercise a greater influence in their own nations" (Second Vatican Council, 1965², no. 15). In addition, the Council also encouraged "a love of rigorously searching for the truth and of maintaining and demonstrating it, together with an honest recognition of the limits of human knowledge" (Second Vatican Council, 1965², no. 15). Anscombe's approach to philosophy reflects these fundamental concerns, and she was doing so before these words were even written. Her dogged and fearless pursuit of truth through the careful linguistic and logical approach of analytical philosophy (a rational approach to truth, I might add, that was closely aligned with and influential in her own British homeland) gave her a unique window into the working of the contemporary mind, one that impacted the English-speaking world and beyond, giving the seekers of truth new insights into the meaning and nature of truth. Her voice was something to be reckoned with, and it did not go unnoticed in the circles of Catholic philosophical and theological thought in search of renewal. It represented the voice of reason, but one that was not inimical to the voice of faith.

As far as her impact on Catholic moral theology is concerned, in 1968, just a few years after the close of the Second Vatican Council, Anscombe gave this astute analysis of the state of moral theology of her day:

For a long time up till recently moral theologians were preoccupied with the question what specific kinds of actions are allowable, in the sense that a man who will do them need not consider himself *ipso facto* excluded from the sacraments. No doubt the aim was to avoid driving people out of the Church. "We want to make money in such-and-such ways, take such-and-such courses of action against one another, do this and that to maintain our position in the world or keep our job: can we consider this to be no sin?" The moral theologian would see if we could. But if this is the growing point of moral theology, then moral theology is developing unhealthily; for such questions are peripheral, and only if they are seen as peripheral can they be intelligently answered. One thing central to moral theology ought to be a sound philosophy of act and intention, which would have to bring this subject matter into connection with the total orientation of a human life and with the virtuous and vicious habits of human beings. For the actions and decisions that are characteristic of a virtue need not be severally obligatory, for a man in whom they are notably lacking to be a bad man.

And again, if these questions are wrongly treated as central, then moral unsoundness results—members of the Church, both clergy and laity, will in general have been getting poor moral instruction and will be at best enfeebled. Moreover, now that people feel dissatisfied and attempt a more positive account of morals, they tend to become mushy. (Anscombe, 1981[9], p. 91)

Anscombe feared that Catholic moral theology was in danger of becoming either "enfeebled" or "mushy." She is here criticizing, on the one hand, the manualist tradition's overemphasis on specific acts, with its overly legalistic attitude toward morality, its focus on obedience to the law, and its tendency to isolate morality from the virtuous life and a person's overall orientation toward God, and, on the other hand, a certain laissez-faire attitude towards morality that was creeping into the cultural mindset of Western society in the 1960s and in the immediate aftermath of the Second Vatican Council. Although she recognizes that it is often necessary to enter into a rigorous analysis of our duties and responsibilities before the law, she insists that such an approach should not be moral theology's central concern. To do so, presents a weak and "enfeebled" approach to moral living, one that focuses on rules and regulations and fails to inspire and give life. She also calls for avoiding the other extreme, which overlooks the law, forgets to draw basic moral distinctions, and makes too facile and "mushy" a connection between what is right and how a person feels. Instead, she calls for moral theology to follow a thoughtful *via media* by rooting itself in "a sound philosophy of act and intention," an area to which she devoted much time and effort and for which she herself was widely recognized as being a provocative and seminal thinker (Oppenheimer, 2011).

It bears noting, moreover, that for Anscombe both virtue ethics and action theory represented an approach to ethics upon which both Catholic and non-Catholic ethicists could agree. Alan Vincelette summarizes her position in this way:

> ...in a secular culture there can at least be an agreement between believer and non-believers about virtues and vices and their contribution to human flourishing; and this constitutes a basis for an objective ethics in which virtues and vices are assessable as good or bad insofar as they contribute to human well-being. (Vincelette, 2011, p. 189)

Similarly, the Catholic moral theology of the day needed to move away from its emphasis on law, duty, and obligation and bring the life of virtue back to the center of consideration. Anscombe's thought represented a sound voice of reason for nudging both philosophical ethics and Catholic moral theology back to an emphasis on virtue.

Conclusion

A few years ago in a piece for the *New York Times* marking the tenth anniversary of her death, Mark Oppenheimer described Anscombe as an "outspoken Catholic philosopher," considered by some "the greatest postwar English philosopher, and the greatest female philosopher ever (a superlative she would loathe)," whose "fearless thinking and uncompromising Christian writing" was "enjoying a renaissance." He further asserts that her views "are inseparable from her biography" (Oppenheimer, 2011).

In considering Anscombe's impact on Catholic moral thought of the post-Vatican II era, I would further assert that her views toward the Christian moral life were shaped by her marriage to Peter Geach and her devotion to her family and to the Catholic faith. As Cardinal Cahal B. Daly said of the couple:

> Peter and Elizabeth have shared a passion for truth which has been intensified by their deep Christian faith....Their contribution to the Church and to the Catholic community in our time has been immense. They have demonstrated that there is a Catholic way of philosophizing, which is still wholly philosophical, at once totally faithful to the laws of reason and the norms of philosophy and to the rigorous demands of logic, and also uncompromisingly loyal to divine Revelation and the teaching of the Catholic Church....They have been pioneers of a genuine renewal of Catholic thought, which, like all authentic renewal, returns to earlier and purer sources, and can therefore

revivify present currents of thought. They have shown that many of what they...found to be aberrations in some contemporary moral theology, written and taught by Catholics, are fundamentally based on philosophical fallacies as well as deviating from Catholic orthodoxy. Elizabeth and Peter, in short, demonstrated that Catholic orthodoxy is philosophically respectable, as well as being a foundational element of integral European humanism. (Daly, 1994, p. viii-ix)

In these remarks, Cardinal Daly puts his finger on the important contribution of renewal that Anscombe has made to Catholic thought in general and Catholic moral thought in particular. Along with her husband and colleague, Peter Geach, she helped do for the Catholic faith on a philosophical level what the *Nouvelle Théologie* (or movement of *Ressourcement*) of the twentieth century did for it on the theological: put it in touch with "earlier, purer sources" deep in the tradition that gave it new insights into the Gospel, and its concrete ramifications for living the Catholic faith in today's world.[6]

Anscombe revivified Catholic moral thought in a variety of ways. She developed a sound philosophy of act and intention that could give moral theology a firm philosophical basis that was both rooted in the tradition and grounded in the intellectual, cultural, and spiritual sensitivities of her day (Anscombe, 1957; Anscombe, 1981[4]; Vincelette, 2011, pp. 186-92). She helped rehabilitate interest in virtue ethics by pointing out the fault lines of the predominant deontological, utilitarian, and consequentialist ethics of modern moral philosophy and which eventually occasioned a corresponding

---

[6]The proponents of the "Nouvelle Théologie" (Yves Congar, Henri de Lubac, Jean Danielou, Henri Bouillard, Louis Boyer, and others) proposed a renewal of Catholic theology by returning to the Scriptural and patristic sources of the faith (the method of "Ressourcement") and were a major influence in the reforms of the Second Vatican Council (1962-65).

paradigmatic shift in focus of Catholic moral thinking from a casuistic emphasis on duty and obligation before natural and divine law to an appreciation of virtue and the particular dispositions of the soul appropriate for the Christian life in the Spirit.[7] She affirmed the existence of intrinsically evil acts determined in total independence from their consequences, while also asserting that some of the key notions of deontological ethics such as *moral* duty and *moral* obligation are obsolete and should be abandoned (Anscombe, 1981[4], pp. 26, 34; Anscombe,1972, pp. 2-3). She conducted a careful analysis of the principle of double effect (or "side effects," as she preferred to call it) and pointed out the weaknesses involved in the attempt of Catholic moral theologians to reinterpret it solely in the light of proportionalist and/or consequentialist thinking (Anscombe, 2005[2], p. 215).[8] She gave new impetus

---

[7]Although the so-called ethical revolution of 1958 has been interpreted in various ways, it is widely held that Anscombe's essay, "Modern Moral Philosophy" (1958), along with the contributions of her Oxford colleague, Philippa Foot, raised the profile of virtue ethics in contemporary philosophical ethics and that their call for a renewed focus on virtue ethics eventually caused Catholic philosophers and moral theologians to take another look at their own rich tradition and refocus their efforts. For Anscombe's place in the return to virtue ethics, see Chappel, 2013, pp. 149-71.

[8]Anscombe builds her analysis of the principle of "double effect" around the thesis that "All human action is moral action. It is either good or bad (It may be both)" (Anscombe, 2005[2], p. 212). She argues that "[t]he idea that a human action could be called a 'pre-moral evil,' or evil in a pre-moral sense, is extremely confused," because "when it is the description of an act of a human being, even though not of a human act, it is still a moral action-description" (Anscombe, 2005[2], p. 215). Anscombe made her remarks on the principle of double effect at a time when the proportionalist controversy was in full swing. She was highly skeptical not only of this theory's claim of having its origins in the thought of Aquinas, but also of its use of language, its analysis of pre-moral evil, and its tendency to deny the existence of intrinsically evil acts. It bears noting that the theory of proportionalism is often linked (however precariously) with the theory of consequentialism (be it "strong" or "soft"; "absolute" or "mixed") and is a term which Anscombe herself coined and a theory of moral action she severely criticized. See Anscombe 1981[4], p. 36.

to the just war theory by showing how it could be applied in concrete situations and by openly criticizing those utilitarian interpretations that sought to justify almost any action in the defense of a greater good (Anscombe, 1981[8]; Anscombe 1981[5]; Vincelette, 2011, 192-93). She argued that all abortion was evil and warned that a nation with "liberal" abortion laws could easily lose respect for the dignity of the human being and rapidly devolve into "a nation of murderers" (Anscombe, 2005[1], p. 73; Geach, 2005, p. xvi). She provided a clear-eyed analysis of the issues revolving around artificial contraception and gave a bold defense of the traditional Catholic position on sexual intercourse at a time when a large number of Catholic moral theologians and a majority of the Catholic faithful (at least in the English-speaking world) held contrary positions in both thought and practice (Anscombe, 1972, pp. 2-3; Oppenheimer, 2011).[9] She did all this—and so very much more—mainly by simply philosophizing, which she saw as

---

[9]In 1972, Anscombe published what has been described as "a deeply unfashionable, and still widely read, argument against birth control" (Oppenheimer, 2011). In it, she affirmed that "Christianity taught that men ought to be as chaste as pagans thought honest women ought to be; the contraceptive morality teaches that women need to be as little chaste as pagans thought men need be." In her argument, she shows how from the very outset Christianity was at odds with the pagan world on such issues as fornication, infanticide, idolatry, and the nature of marriage. Moreover, she points out that "[i]n Christian teaching a value is set on every human life and on men's chastity as well as on women's and this is part of the ordinary calling of a Christian, not just in connection with the austerity of monks. Faithfulness, by which a man turned only to his spouse, forswearing all other women, was counted as one of *the* great goods of marriage." She goes on to say that if contraceptive intercourse is not intrinsically wrong, then it would be very difficult to object to fornication, adultery, or even marriage between people of opposite sexes. She further states that when sexual intercourse is separated from fertility "more and more people will have intercourse with little feeling of responsibility, little restraint, and *yet* they just won't be so careful about always using contraception. And so the widespread use of contraceptives naturally leads to more and more rather than less and less abortion" (Anscombe, 1972, pp. 2-3).

nothing but "thinking about the most difficult and ultimate questions."

By renewing our contact with primary sources ranging from Aristotle to Aquinas to various insights from the tradition of Catholic orthodoxy and by providing us with a studied rational and linguistic analysis of their context and content, Anscombe was able to shed new light on Catholic thought in the areas of fundamental and special moral theology and, in doing so, helped to break up the logjam of controversy in Catholic moral thought of the post-Vatican II era and thus help move the tradition forward. Her impact on Catholic moral thought in the post-Vatican II era was crisp, wide-ranging, and substantial. It is also not yet fully understood and will probably be the subject of some debate for some time to come, as scholars examine the evolution of her thought, discuss some of the subtle differences in her earlier and later writing, and stake out her influence on their thought in a variety of ways.[10] As a Catholic philosopher, she cleared the intellectual landscape of much useless debris and mapped out a coherent *via media* between opposing extremes by raising challenging questions and unearthing previously unnoticed currents of thought that, in time, would give rise to a resurgence of virtue theory in the philosophical and theological circles of her day. Nor was she afraid to get her hands dirty and tackle head-on (and with fearless acumen, I might add) some of the great moral issues of her time. Without her analyses of some of these pressing issues, the Church's moral teachings would have been deprived of a powerful (and fearless) philosophical defense of orthodoxy at a time when it was desperately needed.

---

[10]See, for example, Chappel, 2013, pp.149-71; Matthew B. O'Brien, 2013, pp. 47-56. Anscombe (1981[2], pp. vii-ix) herself recognizes that she has both addressed different audiences in her writings and made certain changes in her argued positions over the years.

References

Anscombe, G. E. M. (1957). Intention. Oxford: Basil Blackwell.

Anscombe, G. E. M. (1972). Contraception and chastity. *The Human World*, 7, 9-30. Retrieved from http://www. orthodoxytoday.org/articles/AnscombeChastity.php (pp. 1-22 printout).

Anscombe, G. E. M. (1981[1]). Faith. In The collected philosophical papers of G.E.M. Anscombe, vol. 3, Ethics, religion and politics (pp. 113-120). Oxford: Basil Blackwell.

Anscombe, G. E. M. (1981[2]). Introduction. In The collected philosophical papers of G.E.M. Anscombe, vol. 3, Ethics, religion and politics (pp. vii-ix). Oxford: Basil Blackwell.

Anscombe, G. E. M. (1981[3]). The justice of the present war examined. In The collected philosophical papers of G.E.M. Anscombe, vol. 3, Ethics, religion and politics (pp. 72-81). Oxford: Basil Blackwell.

Anscombe, G. E. M. (1981[4]). Modern moral philosophy. In The collected philosophical papers of G.E.M. Anscombe, vol. 3, Ethics, religion and politics (pp. 26-42). Oxford: Basil Blackwell.

Anscombe, G. E. M. (1981[5]). Mr. Truman's Degree. In The collected philosophical papers of G.E.M. Anscombe, vol. 3, Ethics, religion and politics (pp. 62-71). Oxford: Basil Blackwell.

Anscombe, G. E. M. (1981[6]). On transubstantiation. In The collected philosophical papers of G.E.M. Anscombe, vol. 3, Ethics, religion and politics (pp. 107-112). Oxford: Basil Blackwell.

Anscombe, G. E. M. (1981[7]). A reply to Mr. C. S. Lewis's argument that 'naturalism' is self-refuting. In The collected philosophical papers of G.E.M. Anscombe, vol. 2, Metaphysics and the philosophy of mind (pp. 224-32). Oxford: Basil Blackwell.

Anscombe, G. E. M. (1981[8]). War and murder. In The collected philosophical papers of G.E.M. Anscombe, vol. 3, Ethics, religion and politics (pp. 51-61). Oxford: Basil Blackwell.

Anscombe, G. E. M. (1981[9]). "You can have sex without children: Christianity and the new offer. In The collected philosophical papers of G.E.M. Anscombe, vol. 3, Ethics religion and politics (pp. 82-96). Oxford: Basil Blackwell.

Anscombe, G. E. M. (2005[1]). The dignity of the human being. In M. Geach and L. Gormally (Eds.), Human life, action and ethics: Essays by G.E.M. Anscombe (pp. 65-73). Exeter, UK: Imprint Academic.

Anscombe, G. E. M. (2005[2]). Action, intention and 'double effect.' In M. Geach and L. Gormally (Eds.), Human life, action and ethics: Essays by G.E.M. Anscombe (pp. 207-26). Exeter, UK: Imprint Academic.

Ascombe, G. E. M. (2008). Twenty opinions common among modern Anglo-American philosophers. In Mary Geach and Luke Gormally (Eds.), Faith in a hard ground (pp. 66-68). Exeter, UK: Imprint Academic.

Anscombe, G. E. M. & Geach, P. (1961). Three philosophers. Ithaca, NY: Cornell University Press.

Catechism of the Catholic Church. (1993). Retrieved from http://www.vatican.va/archive/ENG0015/_INDEX.HTM.

Chappel, T. (2013). Virtue ethics in the twentieth century. In D. C. Russell (Ed.), The Cambridge companion to virtue ethics (pp. 149-77). Cambridge, UK: Cambridge University Press.

Daly, C. B. (1994). Foreword. In L. Gormally (Ed.), Moral truth and moral tradition: Essays in honour of Peter Geach and Elizabeth Anscombe (pp. vii-ix). Dublin: Four Courts Press.

Dolan, J. M. (2001). G. E. M. Anscombe: Living the truth. *First Things*, May. Retrieved from http://www. firstthings. com/article/2007/01/g-e-m-anscombe–living-the-truth- 24.

Frede, D. (2013). The historic decline of virtue ethics. In D. C. Russell (Ed.), The Cambridge companion to virtue ethics (pp. 124-48). Cambridge, UK: Cambridge University Press.

Geach, M. (2005). Introduction. In M. Geach and L. Gormally (Eds.), Human life, action and ethics: Essays by G.E.M. Anscombe (pp. xiii-xxi). Exeter, UK: Imprint Academic.

George, R. P. (2001). Elizabeth Anscombe R. I. P.: One of the twentieth century's most remarkable women. *NRO Weekend*, February 3-4. Retrieved from http://old.national review.com/weekend/philosophy/philosophy-george020301.shtml.

Gilson, E. (1985). History of Christian philosophy in the middle ages (reprint of 1955 ed.). London: Sheed & Ward.

Gormally, L. (1994). Introduction. In L. Gormally (Ed.), Moral truth and moral tradition: Essays in honour of Peter Geach and Elizabeth Anscombe (pp. 1-5). Dublin: Four Courts Press.

Gormally, L., Kietzmann, C., & Torralba, J. M. (2012, 7th version). Bibliography of works by G. E. M. Anscombe. Retrieved from http://www.unav.es/filosofia/jmtorralba/anscombe/G.E.M._Anscombe_Bibliography.htm.

John Paul II. (1988). Christifideles laici, Post-synodal apostolic exhortation on the vocation and the mission of the lay faithful in the church and in the world. Retrieved from http://www.vatican.va/holy_father/john_paul_ii/apost_exhortations/documents/hf_jp-ii_exh_30121988_christifideles-laici_en.html.

John Paul II. (1998). Fides et ratio, Encyclical letter. Retrieved from http://www.vatican.va/holy_father/john_paul_ii/encyclicals/documents/hf_jp-ii_enc_14091998_fides-et- ratio_en.html

Leff, G. (1976). The dissolution of the medieval outlook. New York: Harper Torchbooks.

McGrath, A. (2013). C. S. Lewis: A life. Carol Stream, IL: Tyndale House Publishers.

Morris, J. F. (2010). Fides et ratio and John Paul II's call to catholic philosophers: Orthodoxy and/or the unity of truth. In J. P. Hittinger (Ed.), The vocation of the catholic philosopher: From Maritain to John Paul II (pp. 184-200). Washington, D.C.: American Maritain Association.

O'Brien, M. B. (2013). Elizabeth Anscombe and the new natural law lawyers on intentional action. *National Catholic Bioethics Quarterly*, Spring, 47-56.

Oppenheimer, M. (2011). Renaissance for outspoken catholic philosopher. *New York Times*, January 7. Retrieved from http://www.nytimes.com/2011/01/08/us/08beliefs.html?_r=0.

Pelikan, J. (1984). The vindication of tradition. New Haven/London: Yale University Press.

Pinckaers, S. (1995). The sources of Christian ethics (3rd ed.). M. T. Noble (Trans.). Edinburg: T&T Clark.

Porter, J. (2013) Virtue ethics in the medieval period. In D. C. Russell (Ed.), The Cambridge companion to virtue ethics (pp. 70-91). Cambridge, UK: Cambridge University Press.

Second Vatican Council. (1964). Lumen gentium, Dogmatic constitution on the church. Retrieved from http://www.vatican.va/archive/hist_councils/ii_vatican_council/ documents/vat-ii_const_19641121_lumen-gentium_en.html.

Second Vatican Council. (1965[1]). Dei verbum, Dogmatic constitution on divine revelation. Retrieved from http://www.vatican.va/archive/hist_councils/ii_vatican_council/documents/vat-ii_const_19651118_dei-verbum_en.html

Second Vatican Council. (1965[2]). Optatam totius, Decree on priestly training. Retrieved from http://www.vatican.va/archive/hist_councils/ii_vatican_council/documents/vat- ii_decree_19651028_optatam-totius_en.html.

Vincelette, A. (2011). Recent catholic philosophy: The twentieth century. Milwaukee, WI: Marquette University Press.

Weddell, S. A. (2012). Forming intentional disciples: The path to knowing and following Jesus. Huntington, IN: Our Sunday Visitor.

4. Clarifying Anscombe's Ethical Absolutism

Justin Anderson

With renowned brevity, Elizabeth Anscombe lists "Twenty Opinions Common among Modern Anglo-American Philosophers" (2008) in a short paper entitled the same. These twenty theses share, at least in Anscombe's mind, the following three characteristics. First, they are theses "very often" held either implicitly or explicitly by analytic philosophers. Second, they are theses inimical to the Christian religion. Lastly, and here I quote the closing sentence of that brief paper: "Each of them is a philosophical error and can be argued to be such on purely philosophical grounds" (Anscombe, 2008, p. 68). Now, the eighth thesis on Anscombe's list reads: "There are no absolute moral prohibitions which are always in force."[1] In this paper, I aim to elucidate Anscombe's understanding of ethical absolutes by arguing that a more accurate understanding

---

[1] It bears repeating that this is a statement that Anscombe thinks to be wrong. She is not supporting its veracity.

exists in the work of some explicitly Catholic ethicists than by analytic philosophers even of an Anscombean bent.

Arguing for this thesis will involve me in the unpleasant business of taking exception with the account of moral absolutes presented in two of Anscombe's expositors: Roger Teichmann and Duncan Richter. What is worse is that these two are the *only* two Anscombean exegetes I know to have issued book-length expositions of Anscombe's philosophy. I give Teichmann the lead here, but consider Richter to be more at fault. After laying out the former's presentation, I critique it. Finally, I attempt to demonstrate how an Anscombean notion of intentional object can both be found in and potentially illuminate Catholic ethical discussions.

The Teichmann Analysis and Its Insufficiencies

Teichmann's direct analysis of Anscombean absolutism is rather brief. I want to highlight two principal points. First, Teichmann indicates that Anscombe's absolutism is not a mere rule following in a practice. For Anscombe, thinks Teichmann, to know a rule is also to know both (a) its interpretation and (b) its application (or non-application) in a particular case. Simply put, to really know an absolute moral rule, one must have the kind of knowledge of it that gives one the circumstantial awareness Aristotle advocates. Thus, the rules themselves are not all that is necessary. But, alas, Teichmann's Anscombe has argued, for other reasons, that exceptionless generalizations are all we have. Consequently, we cannot be blindly guided by these rules of conduct, for, depending on the circumstance, the rules need interpreting and it may even be permissible to break them.

However, and this is the second point, Teichmann rightly is not satisfied with speaking of absolutes as generalized rules. Therefore, he avers that for Anscombe the source of such absolutes is the character traits of the virtuous person in the Aristotelian mold that enables and motivates one to ask whether some proposed act is just. Thus, while we only have imperfect generalized moral rules for Teichmann's Anscombe, still there are some actions which will be discounted for the virtuous person.

> So what is the source of Anscombe's absolutism? It is to Aristotle, once again, that we must turn. Whereas a consequentialist asks, 'Would doing X maximize good consequences?', a virtuous person in the Aristotelian mould will ask such questions as, 'Would doing X be just?' Wanting to ask that question, and counting it as being in X's favour that it is just (if it is), means having a certain character trait, a certain settled disposition of character. Anscombe's view is that the trait in question will involve ruling certain things out... (2008, p. 121)

Two aspects of this presentation of Anscombe's absolutism are worth a moment's pause. The first point is Teichmann's assertion that Anscombean absolutism must include the knowledge that is capable of perceiving how the absolute rule applies or is interpreted within a particular situation. That is, the Aristotelian virtuous character needs to take account of particular circumstances to understand how an absolute should be interpreted or whether one can dispense with that absolute altogether. One can find this explanation at least initially odd, because it seems to be the exact opposite of what Anscombe famously holds when she wrote, among other places, at the end of "Modern Moral Philosophy:"

> ...but if someone really thinks *in advance* that it is open to question whether such an action as procuring the judicial execution of the innocent should be quite excluded from consideration – I do not want to argue with him; he shows a corrupt mind. (Anscombe, 1958, p. 191)

I want to stress, I do not think these two statements – the one of Teichmann, the other of Anscombe – to be irreconcilable in themselves. I simply say, it could strike one as interesting that Teichmann wants Anscombe's absolutism to square the ideas that (a) the discernment of whether or not an absolute rule applies in some current case given that case's particularities and circumstances, *with* (b) Anscombe's words that there are some acts that one cannot be open to "in advance" and remain an uncorrupted mind. Perhaps these two statements could be reconciled *if certain distinctions are drawn*.

My second point regarding Teichmann's account is that he fails to make those requisite distinctions and that this omission runs the risk of obscuring the true nature of Anscombe's absolutism. Of the distinctions Teichmann might have drawn, the most important is that between what I will call below "rules of conduct" and "rules of intentional acts."[2] By rules of conduct I mean a rule or norm that is understood to forbid certain external performances; and by rules of intentional acts I mean a rule or norm that is understood to forbid certain intentional actions. I will say more about what I mean by these two kinds of absolute norms below. He nowhere corrects his reduction of Anscombe's absolutism to "rules of conduct," but I do think one can read such a distinction in his account if already aware of it. He only asserts the necessity of "an ability to interpret and apply a practical rule is a necessary part of properly grasping such a rule" (p.120).

Such is Teichmann's omission. He may very well understand Anscombe's absolutism as I will argue one ought. Nevertheless,

---

[2] I do think Teichmann's account hints at this sort of distinction when he writes, "A rule of conduct will invoke a category or concept – 'lying, say, or 'murder' – and anyone who follows a rule of conduct will need to ask, in any concrete situation, such a question as 'Would doing X be a case of lying?' They will need to *interpret* the rule in question" (Teichmann, 2008, p.120 – Emphasis in original). But the distinction is not clear. This lack of clarity is what seems to lead Richter astray.

one of the most crucial distinctions necessary to make this conception clear in the mind of the reader is not present in his account. Richter, writing his own account of Anscombe's absolutism and explicitly following Teichmann's account, falls between the holes created by Teichmann's omission. To see this it is worth quoting Richter at length. He writes,

> Probably the main objection to moral absolutism is its apparent inflexibility or inability to deal reasonably with exceptional cases. ...But, according to Teichmann, absolutism need not imply otherwise. Grasping a practical rule properly means being able to interpret and apply it in different situations, he says. No rule can specify all the possible circumstances that would prevent its application, so rules against such things as breaking promises will always tend to be simple and unqualified, even though these rules will not apply in every case and may be broken in some cases where they do apply.... There need not, and perhaps cannot, be any principled specification of what these cases are.... The absolutism that says 'promises must be kept' is therefore not as absolute as it might sound.... The absolutist, on the other hand, rules out some actions as a matter of course. Exceptional circumstances might prompt reconsideration, but some things are simply not options in normal circumstances. (Richter, 2011, pp. 58-59)

Richter confirms this interpretation in the (fallacious) claim that Anscombe accepted promises as an absolute prohibition. However, nowhere does Anscombe claim such.[3] Indeed, by the time one finishes Richter's presentation, one finds that Anscombe's absolutism is only an absolutism "in normal circumstances." Simply put, it is no absolutism at all.

---

[3] I am grateful to Candace Vogler to pointing this out to me in an earlier version of this paper.

Perhaps someone might object that I am being a bit harsh on Teichmann and Richter. Are both not clearly writing of the actual codified rules and not of the acts? To which I could respond, that while one can read Teichmann's account to be merely about the rules and not intentional acts, the distinction itself never appears to compel the reader to understand Anscombe's absolutism as such. As for Richter's account, it seems absolutism can *only* mean absolutism of rules of conduct, which are, for completely correct reasons, softened and dismissed by the end of his explanation. (Below I will return to explain why Richter is correct that Anscombe is willing to dismiss absolute rules of conduct in particular cases, while incorrect that Anscombe's absolutism is a qualified absolutism.)

What then do I wish Teichmann and Richter would have written so as to better represent Anscombe's ethical absolutism? It seems a fitting place to return to the distinction I briefly mentioned above. This distinction is between rules of conduct and rules of intentional action; because, by the nature of language, these two very different kinds of rules can easily appear identical. An absolutist account of rules of conduct might *prima facie* look like an absolutist account of intention actions. This confusion is complicated by the fact that when a rule of conduct becomes a norm which influences one's intentional act, the rule of conduct can be said to be an intentional act.[4] One way of getting at the difference between the two forms of absolutism from within Anscombe's works is what she first considers when she proposes her renowned water pumper example in *Intention* §23. This is the difference between assigning a description to an action of what happens

---

[4] I am grateful to Víctor Velarde-Mayol for bringing this to my attention. Naturally, even though a rule of conduct becomes that which informs an intentional action, that rule of conduct is not the same as *a rule of* intentional action. The rule of conduct forbids a physical conduct, while the rule of intentional action forbids an object of intentional action.

and discerning the description under which an agent intentionally did some action. Regarding "what" happens, Anscombe writes,

> Now we ask: What is this man doing? What is *the* description of his action? First, of course, any description of what is going on, with him as subject, which is in fact true. E.g. he is earning wages, he is supporting his family, he is wearing away his shoe-soles, he is making a disturbance of the air. (2000, §23, p. 37)

Any of these descriptions can be right descriptions of some performed action. However, Anscombe goes on to show how these sorts of answers fail to provide the key: intentional action. She continues, "However, our enquiries into the question 'Why?' enable us to narrow down our consideration of descriptions of what he is doing to a range covering all and only his intentional actions" (Ibid). Not only are these distinct for Anscombe, but there is a danger in confusing external conduct and intentional action. She echoes this warning in several places, but here is one:

> This shews once more, that you cannot take any performance (even an interior performance) as itself an act of intention; for if you describe a performance, the fact that it has taken place is not a proof of intention; words for example may occur in somebody's mind without his meaning them. (2000, §27, p. 49)

That which is done intentionally is not only done, but done under a particular description. This pairs nicely with what Anscombe writes about the object of intentional action. "We must always remember that an object is not what what-is-aimed-at *is*; the description *under which* it is aimed at is that under which it is *called* the object" (2000, §35, p.66 – emphasis in original).[5] Therefore, using Anscombe's own words in the last passage as my key, I am going to specify my complaint that both Teichmann and Richter present Anscombe as an absolutist about rules that prohibit certain external conducts as being off-limits (performance-absolutism), when they should have presented Anscombe as an absolutist about rules that prohibit certain objects of intentional action as being off-limits (object-absolutism). This would have enabled them to retain her absolutist stance without either ignoring her philosophical nuances or destroying her absolutism. The principal difference between the two sorts of absolutisms is that according to object-absolutism one is not primarily discerning whether the present case is an exception to the rule or not, but whether the proposed act is (or is not) the kind that is prohibited by the rule. This is precisely why I stated that Teichmann's account could be read according to my distinction though it is still ambiguous, but Richter's account could not.

Moreover, in the account provided by some object-absolutists, like that of Aquinas, the circumstances surrounding a situation may alter the description under which an agent performs his or her intentional act. In such cases, what looks like a circumstance has ceased to be such and actually becomes part of the object of the intentional action (IaIIae q. 18, a. 10).[6] Thus, object-absolutism can take account of all the pressures of abnormal "circumstances" without needing to claim an exception to the rule or norm: the object of the intentional action has changed. This is why Richter is actually completely correct to hold that

---

[5]I understand this passage as being able to be paraphrased thus: "We must always remember that an object is not the thing at which one aims; instead the description *under which* one aims at the thing *is called* the object."

[6]All subsequent such reference notes refer to Thomas Aquinas's *Summa Theologiae* unless otherwise noted.

sometimes, because of extraordinary "circumstances," there can be an exception to an absolute rule. But he is wrong to think this means that there is an exception to the object forbidden. It, therefore, would have been more accurate for him to hold that a rule does not come to bear on the act performed, because the object of the intentional action lies outside the purview of the absolute rule. Consequently, performance-absolutism – which measures merely external, physical actions *and* in so doing ignores the idea of action done under different descriptions, and hence is incapable of taking account of objects in human action – is forced to acknowledge there can be exceptions to the absolute rule. If this is the only sense of absolutism to which one holds, then it can very well seem that one's absolutism is not actually absolute. Conversely, with object-absolutism – which does not merely look to the physical description of the act, but to the object of the intentional act (or "from the perspective of the acting person") – one can understand an absolute prohibition against the kind of act that is being performed (John Paul II, 1993, §78, quoted in Brock 2008).

Before moving to the next section, it bears repeating that Teichmann is doing several things well. He does treat one's expression of moral absolutes. More importantly, he does address the requisite (but not sufficient) character traits one must possess to rightly identify certain acts as prohibited regardless of circumstances.[7] Nevertheless, Teichmann's presentation seems to conflate the physical conduct with the object of intentional action and, thereby, commits the error Anscombe warns against in *Intention* §35. In fairness to Teichmann, there is a reason he could not have directly pointed to the full grounding of Anscombe's absolutism. Simply put, Anscombe was adamant that contemporary

---

[7]However, on object-absolutism it becomes all the more convincing that an excellence of discernment is requisite.

philosophical ethics does not have the conceptual baggage for the journey; and Teichmann's brief account ends on that remark. However, by reducing Anscombe's absolutism to a performance-absolutism and not raising the issue of an object-absolutism the reader is left with the impression that Anscombe's absolutism could permit exceptions. This is precisely the trap into which Richter's presentation tumbles. Slowly, Anscombe's absolutism becomes no absolutism at all.

Anscombe among Contemporary Catholic Ethicists

In light of Anscombe's statement of the lack of philosophical baggage possessed by contemporary ethics to make sense of moral absolutes, I want to make the fairly obvious move of arguing that there does exist the philosophical baggage by which one might provide an account for object-absolutism in another tradition coexisting with contemporary philosophical ethics. I am referring to the Catholic intellectual tradition, and in particular that of the contemporary Thomistic-minded scholars. Working within that tradition, I want to examine especially the work of Rev. Martin Rhonheimer and Rev. Kevin L. Flannery, S.J.[8]

---

[8]Both are Catholic priests working as moral philosophers in the Pontifical university system in Rome, Italy. Both receive, in my rough estimation, more attention from Catholic theologians and Catholics working in moral philosophy than does Anscombe. Moreover, both have acknowledged in different ways some use or familiarity with Anscombe. Describing his own relationship to Anscombe's works in 2009, Flannery explicitly calls himself "not being an 'Anscombe expert;' but (shall we say) a friendly admirer" (Flannery, 2009, p. 39). Rhonheimer has cited Anscombe in various works, but uses explicitly Anscombe's formulation cited above from §35 of *Intention* regarding the object of an act as a confirmation of his own view on moral object. I will visit Rhonheimer's context of this passage below, so it is omitted here. Also worthy of note in this regard, but a scholar I will not explicitly consider, is Rev. Stephen L. Brock to whom Flannery often defers and also has to some extent engaged Anscombe's works. See (Brock, 1998).

Central to the ethicists of the Catholic intellectual tradition's discussion of moral absolutism is the conception of moral object, typically identified with the work of Thomas Aquinas.[9] Now, Anscombe nowhere addresses the issue of moral object. This is true of even her more explicitly Catholic writings. (Though, granted, she at times comes close, these references are fleeting.) Therefore, while it would be illicit to assume Anscombe had something like a conception of moral object in mind when working out her absolutism, nevertheless it is not outside the realm of real possibility. Indeed, it is even very plausible. Part of the reason for this is that there seems simply no other philosophical concepts that operate as "moral object" does. If there were such an alternative idea, then it would need to furnish the grounds, not for why some action is wrong (e.g. appeal to divine law, etc.), but to establish a framework whereby an act would be a certain sort of act and not another. Furthermore, it would be interesting to know why it is not merely an alternative conception of the moral object, which has enjoyed a venerable tradition by a predominant moral absolutist intellectual tradition.[10]

It will profit our project in two ways to look at the lines traced by Flannery and Rhonheimer on the moral object. First, it will establish a more explicit manner of thinking of the moral

---

[9] The reader will carefully note that Anscombe's absolutism was dubbed an "object-absolutism" not because of the occurrence of the term in Aquinas and the Catholic tradition, but because of her own use of the word in *Intention*. It might be considered a happy coincidence the term is taken up by both sets of scholars. But even if the term were thought to mean something completely other than as it appears in the Thomistic tradition, then one would still need to argue that Anscombe had nothing like *objectum* in her philosophical repertoire. But that she did was the first point of this essay.

[10] Candace Vogler's reference to the analytic tradition's "act-types" as a similar notion is one current possibility. However, it is worth noting how quickly it can be compared and contrasted to the "moral object" of the Catholic intellectual tradition. It is unclear if the slight differences that exist between these two concepts are capable of doing two different things in a moral theory. Cf. (Vogler, 2013, pp. 245-246).

object which, if it *did* not, *could* certainly underlie Anscombe's object-absolutism. In this way, one will see what kind of philosophical forays regarding object-absolutism Catholic scholars are capable of making because they have access to philosophical baggage given them by the wider Catholic (and classical western philosophical) intellectual tradition. Second, these preliminary traces will occasion the opportunity to reflect on how an Anscombean account of intention might be able to aid the Thomistic conception of the moral object in further establishing its own philosophical account of an object-absolutist ethic. On the basis of Anscombe's profound contributions to philosophical concepts, especially that of intention, that are employed by the Catholic tradition in its discussion of the moral object, there should be little doubt that some fruit could be gathered from such a dialogue.

Both Flannery's and Rhonheimer's explanation of the moral object highlight some broad lines of agreement. Most central is the basic understanding that the moral object is that which renders an act to be of a certain kind. In the Aristotelian-Thomistic locution, the moral object gives a human act its species.

The use of this term species signals a second harmony in the two accounts. Both authors explicitly value Aquinas's use of language of the natural universe (i.e. form and matter) in describing the contours of the moral universe. Nevertheless, both philosophers acknowledge that the analogical use of this language must be performed cautiously if one is to avoid grave mistakes. For example, a common error arises when one thinks physically, or more precisely, when one thinks about the physical dimensions of moral acts in an improper manner (Flannery, 2003, pp. 117-118; Rhonheimer, 2011, n.2). And so, while keeping these two universes separate, natural and moral, Flannery and Rhonheimer import the language of the natural world to speak of the moral world (i.e. matter and form, object, etc.). And for this reason the phrase "moral object" is used in lieu of simply "object."

These philosophers also follow the broad stroke of Aquinas in making the distinction between "the interior object of the will" and the "exterior object" in every moral act (IaIIaeq. 18, a. 6, c). In this framework, and employing the hylomorphic language, it is the interior object of the will that acts as the form, while the exterior object is the material about (*materia circa quam*) which the form is brought to bear. The devilish details lie for many Thomistic moral philosophers and theologians in how to understand what Aquinas is referring to in this distinction and how to properly understand this relationship between interior and exterior object.

As a final note both authors emphasize that regardless of the precise relationship between interior and exterior object, formal and material aspect of the moral object, the central role of shaping an act to be the kind of act that it is falls to reason.[11]

It is important to emphasize that both Flannery and Rhonheimer have different methodologies and different ways of reading Aquinas, especially in regard to the moral object. Their differing methodologies, Flannery typically seeing Aquinas as highly Aristotelian, have led to differences in account. Within these differences, Rhonheimer has distinguished himself for a position not commonly held among other scholars. Though because more might agree with Flannery's conclusions, it does not mean they would agree with his general method.

Flannery goes into Aristotle to find grounds for moral absolutism and, working from the *Nicomachean Ethics* II.6,

---

[11] There are strong differences between these authors. Flannery following Stephen L. Brock (1998) will speak of the formal object and the material object, while Rhonheimer insists that there is only one object with a dual dimension. Cf. (Rhonheimer, 2011, p. 470, n. 59). I have followed Rhonheimer in his use of the material and formal as aspects of the single moral object. This is more for convenience of expression for this essay rather than a philosophical justification of his position contra Brock's and Flannery's.

concludes that moral absolutes depend on the intelligible natures of the moral universe (Flannery, 2003, p. 97). This moral universe, argues Flannery, is distinct from the natural universe insofar as the former is populated by intentional acts and the latter by things. Flannery also thinks that reason plays a foundational role in shaping one's act. His emphasis is placed on reason's capacity to determine intentional acts to be of various kinds. This is clearly in contrast to the role human reason takes up in regard to the natural universe where, in the Aristotelian-Thomistic understanding, natural entities are already determined to be a single kind of thing by their form. Reason takes up no such role in the natural universe. That which issues from reason is an object, but this is a moral object that renders the act to be the kind of act that it is. Herein, Flannery becomes more Thomistic. Flannery also thinks that the role of "object" is a privileged door into Aquinas's world of ethics from contemporary philosophical ethics (Ibid).

Rhonheimer, for his part, notes with Aquinas and Aristotle that that which an act aims at can be thought of in two ways: as the end itself (as in the thing itself, where the end of the act is the thing itself) and as the possession of the end (IaIIae q. 16, a. 3). Now the moral object, that which gives an intentional act its species, is not constituted by the physical thing (the end itself), but by the *ratio boni*, the aspect of good under which the end is willed. Rhonheimer is emphatic on this point contra other Thomistic scholars: the species of the act is determined not by the willed thing itself (*res volita*), but by the will's relation to the end as proposed to it by reason. His particular understanding of reason's role in specifying the moral act is precisely why Rhonheimer can quote Anscombe with approval in his exposé regarding the moral object. Rhonheimer writes:

That is why the *objective* content of human actions can be expressed each time only in an intentional description of the corresponding action. 'What' we do is always a 'why' we do something *on purpose*. It is a 'material doing' (*'materia circa quam'*) chosen *under a description,* while it is the 'description' which actually contains the intentional content of the action. That is why it seems to me correct when Elizabeth Anscombe writes: 'We must always remember that....' (Rhonheimer, 2008, p. 61)

Thus, Rhonheimer speaks of the moral object being "the end of a deliberately willed act" or "the end of an act proceeding from deliberate will," but he opposes others' descriptions of the moral object as "a deliberately willed end." The formal object is the *'ratio boni'* (the description under which something is chosen). The material object is the *'res volita'* (the end itself which is chosen). Together formal and material aspects of an intentional action constitute the moral object. In fact, to mistake the moral object for the thing chosen (*res volita*) or letting that aspect determine the moral object is what, in Rhonheimer's estimation, constitutes one's conception of the moral object as "physicalist."

A brief aside on physicalism and its opposite, intentionalism. Both terms are used within this debate generally in a pejorative manner. There are various senses one attributes to the terms as well.[12] However, as I am using them here "physicalism" is the accusation that one's conversant is identifying the moral object too much or in an improper way with the physical object (or

---

[12]Brock addresses the most popular two senses of the term "physicalism": "The senses are at least two. Sometimes it refers to a way of establishing moral norms. In this sense, it means, roughly, an uncritical use of a physical entity or nature as a criterion for judging moral goodness and badness. At other times the word refers to a way of conceiving the items to which moral goodness and badness belong: human acts. It then means, again roughly, an undue reduction of human acts to their physical features, with too little weight given to the role played in their constitution by factors such as intention, or choice, or reason" (Brock, 2008, p. 1).

"thing" where there is a thing) of the action. Naturally, such a conception is usually thought to not accurately acknowledge the subjective dimension of the moral object, like its being constituted by intention. Conversely, "intentionalism" is the accusation that one's conversant is identifying the moral object too much or in an improper way with the intention of the agent. Consequently, this understanding is usually thought to not accurately acknowledge the objective dimension of the moral object (i.e. that, using Anscombe's expression, one's intention can become the matter of "making such a little speech to oneself" about what is and what is not one's intention). I will return to this language of "physicalist" and "intentionalist" in the next section in order to understand, based on Anscombe's book *Intention*, how one might conceive of the moral object. This light could potentially not only further clarify the grounding of her object-absolutism, but also aid the ethicist working inside the Catholic intellectual tradition to illuminate in what way one may accept intention as constitutive of the moral object, while not succumbing to an understanding of intention which is altogether locked away from its third-party observer.

Thomas Aquinas, whose works Rhonheimer generally engages with, explicitly makes the point that the specification of the moral object comes not from the material object, but the formal object. This is precisely, argues Rhonheimer, why a sin of pride can manifest itself in a great many different material acts and still remain the same species of sin: pride (Rhonheimer, 2011, p. 487, and Flannery, 2013, pp. 83-84). As for the formal aspect of the moral object, it is that which is conceived by reason and presented to the will to be chosen. Hence, for Rhonheimer reason plays a critical role in specifying the moral object of an act. It goes without saying that Rhonheimer's understanding of the moral object has been considered dangerous and labeled that of an intentionalist. Interestingly, Rhonheimer argues that to be a physicalist is the same foundation which led many to proportionalism, which in Catholic moral speak is very often understood to be a mere form of consequentialism (Rhonheimer, 2011, pp. 498-506, and John Paul II, 1993, §75). Flannery also lays critical emphasis on reason's role in shaping the moral object. Nevertheless, his Thomistic analysis of the moral object differs from Rhonheimer's in at least one crucial issue: the role of the material aspect in the definition of moral object. Flannery does not think reason (as formal aspect) is the *only* thing that shapes the moral object and this attention to the material aspect limits the degree to which his conception of moral object can be understood as intentionalist.

Prospects of an Anscombean Treatment of the Moral Object

Before one turns to Anscombe for a contemporary account of moral object at least three preliminary questions present themselves. First, why seek something from Anscombe on the moral object? And even if one can seek such a concept, then how might she work on such a concept in her native contemporary analytic philosophy? Finally, if her native philosophical landscape is taken up, then what are the promises and perils of working out such an Anscombean account?

Regarding the first question, it makes sense to look towards Anscombe's texts on objects of intentional action and act-types for clarity on the nature of the moral object because there is confusion regarding the topic in contemporary Catholic philosophy and theology. Too often the debate among ethicists working in the Catholic intellectual tradition, Thomists or not, gets bogged down in textual interpretative questions of Aquinas, which is often seen as the only way to clarify the nature of the moral object. To some, like Christopher Kaczor, the texts of Aquinas on moral object, though not permitting any position, do *not* conclusively endorse any single contemporary interpretation. Kaczor writes of the current situation,

I wonder if it might be the case that the texts of Thomas dealing with these matters do not lend themselves to answering the questions that are being posed. I do think, and Jensen shows, that the texts of Aquinas, cannot support proportionalism. But in terms of adjudicating between the views of Rhonheimer, Brock, Long, Flannery, and Finnis on the specification of the object of the human act, I wonder if the texts of Aquinas are open, legitimately open, to a variety of plausible interpretations which – though incompatible with each other – are reasonably credible readings of the Angelic Doctor. (Kaczor, 2012, pp. 324)

In such a situation, another philosophical voice who has done unique and, indeed, groundbreaking work on such philosophical terms of reference as "intention" may be a worthy dialogue partner.

However, Anscombe is not simply any contemporary voice that might speak to the contemporary Catholic discussion on moral object and more specifically intention's role in shaping the moral object. Many of Anscombe's inspirations issued from, as is more and more frequently explicitly recognized, an engagement with the texts of Aquinas. Candace Vogler writes, "Anscombe was a Thomist. It is very hard to say what kind of Thomist she was" (2013, p.240). Vogler quotes the following passage from Mary Geach, Anscombe's daughter and her literary executor,

Anscombe drew upon [Aquinas's] thought to an unknowable extent: she said to me that it aroused prejudice in people to tell them that a thought came from him: to my sister she said that to ascribe a thought to him made people boringly ignore the philosophical interest of it, whether they were for Aquinas or against him. (Geach, 2011, p. xv)

Geach in another place writes of her mother's methodology,

Did she consider philosophical questions simply for the sake of the theology? Sometimes she would do just the opposite. She devised a method, which she recommended to me, of mining Aquinas for helpful philosophical points: this was to prospect for philosophically useable bits in the *Summa theologiae* by considering to what Catholic doctrine her particular philosophical problem was relevant. (Geach, 2008, p. xiv)

Moreover, it was Anscombe who wrote perhaps the single greatest treatise on intentional action in the modern era. Though, as will be indicated below, approaching Anscombe in this regard should be done only with due caution for the Thomist, nevertheless the result of such an encounter could be quite positive for Catholic moral thought.

Given the obvious – namely, Anscombe's analytic approach to philosophy – *how* can this rapport come about? What Anscombean notions are the most salient to employ in the service of the moral object? Vogler indicates that the notion of "act-type" is the closest concept to Aquinas's *objectum*. Indeed, continues Vogler, "It seems likely that Anscombe had Aquinas's *objectum* in mind when introducing act-types into analytic philosophy" (2013, p. 245).

Vogler goes on to point out four ways act-types in analytic practical philosophy differ from Aquinas's *objectum*. Each of the four variances are traceable to the general "inherent unfriendliness" of analytic philosophy to speak about actual psychological, internal events of intellect and will without due reference to external evidence. This sort of concern in Anscombe presents her own approach in *Intention*, by isolating responses to a certain form of the question "why" in defining intention itself. This philosophical method is something quite separate from a Thomistic analogous employment of the hylomorphic language to speak of the moral fabric of the world: formal and material aspects of the moral objects of intentional acts. This difference represents both a danger and a promise in engaging an Anscombean account of moral object for the contemporary Catholic ethicist.

The danger of the investigation is that the differences between the two philosophical approaches will be missed, ignored, or simply given too little weight. Intractable disputes are likely between analytic philosophers and more traditional Thomistic thinkers. And yet it is precisely because the two philosophical approaches vary in method that the possibility for a stronger philosophical argument, away from the usual Thomistic textual conundrums, emerges. When one recalls that Anscombe drew from Aquinas, perhaps precisely on the issue of *objectum*, and came to her own insights including various philosophical ways to make similar, if not identical, points, then why can't one draw from Anscombe for clarity on the issue of the *objectum* of an intentional, human acts? While a comparison between Anscombe and Aquinas will involve itself in interpretative difficulties (at least concerning Aquinas's texts), nevertheless a comparison between Anscombe's account and that of contemporary accounts of authors like Jensen, Brock, Rhonheimer, Flannery, et al. may offer insight into which gets at reality better. Herein lies the most pertinent discussion to have and the one I am suggesting. Moreover, the project will be devoid of the different textual readings of Aquinas and may hold appeal for a wider contemporary audience. The establishment of a contemporary philosophical account of moral object serves, as far as I can see, as a key concept in constructing a contemporary philosophical account of ethical absolutes. While there may be even non-philosophical causes for the general denial of an ethical absolutism by contemporary academics, such an inquiry as the one that is already underway could revive the discussion in a meaningful manner.

Having already highlighted the difficulties between an intentionalist and physicalist reading of the moral object in the writings of contemporary ethicists in Catholic dialogue, I want to risk the dangers highlighted above, not to work out an entire Anscombean approach to the moral object, but to distill where Anscombe's text, especially the text of *Intention*, might have put her on the spectrum between the extremes of physicalism and intentionalism as I have generally delineated them. This last task will also serve another purpose: it will further aid in clarifying the kind of ethical absolutism Anscombe holds. As of yet I have only argued that an object-absolutism is tied to the objects of intentional action. If I leave the argument there, then I have done so at the risk of making Anscombe appear to be more on the side of an intentionalism, than is actually the case. Therefore, this last task will at least serve to better indicate the subtly of her account concerning the relation between one's intention in acting and one's performance of an act.

An Anscombean Position on the Intentionalist-Physicalist Spectrum

Anscombe argues that the realm of intention is among those acts not known to the agent by observation. One knows one's intention without observational knowledge (1957, §8, 16). However, neither should this mean that intention is something equated to a mental causality (Ibid. §9-11, 16). There are, she reasons, non-voluntary actions that are mental causalities. As intention is something of the voluntary, then there must be some other aspect of intention that marks it off from *merely* being mental causality (Ibid. §7, 16). This second point is a rather important one. It means that while being knowable by non-observational means, intention is not *only* knowable by non-observational means. It is simply knowable *to the agent* by non-observational means. From the beginning of the work, Anscombe has wanted to get at how it is one knows an agent's intention (Ibid. §4).[13]

Wishing to discover another's intention in acting, we might first ask "What is this man doing?" When the "what" question is asked a wide berth of acceptable answers opens. This is so because when we do act X, we are, in fact, doing a great many things. The "what" question can be answered in a great variety of ways (Ibid. §6, 22-23).[14] However, asking a "why" question – such as "Why is this man doing X?" – constricts the previous wide berth of valid responses to a narrower range of possible answers. When we ask such why questions, thinks Anscombe, we are pursuing the intention of the agent. Nevertheless, it typically is only when the agent himself replies to this sort of "why" question, presuming he is responding sincerely, does the external observer have knowledge of the agent's *actual* intention, his intention in acting. Now, the fact that the actual intention is discovered in the response of the agent indicates that one's intention is, in some way, hidden to the external observer.

_____

[13] Anscombe lists several reasons why it "easily seems that in general the question what a man's intentions are is only authoritatively settled by him." Then she concludes this paragraph stating: "All this conspires to make us think that if we want to know a man's intentions it is into the contents of his mind, and only into these that we must enquire; and hence, that if we wish to understand what intention is, we must be investigating something whose existence is purely in the sphere of the mind; and that although intention issues in actions, and the way this happens also presents interesting questions, still what physically takes place, i.e. what a man actually does, is the very last thing we need consider in our enquiry. Whereas I wish to say that it is the first." While there may be more than one reason for Anscombe's wish to make one's external performance the first thing inquired about in investigating intentions, one potential reason is her own philosophical tradition being "inherently unfriendly to acts of intellect or acts of will" which is "predicated upon distancing itself from focus on actual psychological processes…" (Vogler, 2013, p. 245).
[14] This is why a great many things can be said to be foreseen without being intended.

That is to say, when asked 'Why did you replenish the house supply with poisoned water?' he might either reply 'I couldn't care tuppence' or say 'I was glad to help to polish them off', and if capable of saying what had actually occurred in him at the time as the vehicle of either of these thoughts, he might have to say only that he grunted. This is the kind of truth there is in the statement 'Only you can know if you had such-and-such an intention or not'. There is a point at which only what the man himself says is a sign; and here there is room for much dispute and fine diagnosis of his genuineness. (Ibid. §25)

This conclusion seems to validate the claim that Anscombe would agree with a more intentionalist reading of the moral object, and this account would be based immediately on her understanding of intention.

Nevertheless, there are crucial passages in *Intention* where it would seem an Anscombean account of moral object would have to reject such an intentionalist reading of the moral object. Anscombe is absolutely opposed to making a man's intention completely hidden in every instance from external observation. She returns to her notion of intention to re-emphasize that it is not something unknowable from external observation. To put it another way, simply because an agent's intention is (a) known to the agent by non-observational knowledge, and (b) revealed to external observers by his or her sincere responses to such "why" questions, it does not follow that there are no circumstances in which the agent's intention is *completely* unknowable by external observation. Anscombe writes, "A man's intention in acting is not so private and interior a thing that he has absolute authority in saying *what* it is – as he has absolute authority in saying *what* he dreamt" (Ibid. §22 – emphasis in original).

Again, the reason for this is because, for Anscombe, one's intention is something knowable to the agent by a non-observational form of knowledge, while still not being identical to mental causality. Yet, if the realm of things that are *only* knowable by non-observational knowledge is the same as those of mental causality, then intention not being identical to mental causality means that intention is not wholly identifiable with that which can only be known by non-observational knowledge. An Anscombean account of intention defies the notion that it cannot be known apart from the perspective of the acting person. Under the right circumstances it certainly can.

The same point is laid bare in another way during her famed treatise on intention. Anscombe summarizes her thoughts by stating that intentional action is that action to which one can respond to the question "why," asked in a particular sense of the question. Yet, these responses, to be authentic revelations of intentions, must include one of the following: (a) mention of some future state of affairs, if the mentioning of the future state of affairs can be brought about by the action being performed; (b) giving an interpretation of the action; (c) mention of past history, if this mentioning appeals to some notion of good or harm or further questioning discovers the response is connected to an interpretative motive (intention with which). Such is Anscombe's understanding of intentional action. Why is this important? Because it demonstrates that insofar as there is even a single condition for a response to count as an authentic response to the inquiry into one's intention, then an agent's intention is not something completely locked away from observable knowledge.

Based on Anscombe's analysis of intentional action *in some circumstances* intentions can be known by external observation and perhaps even known with greater certitude than the agent knows them. Intentions are not *completely* the private knowledge of the agent. However, in elucidating the knowledge one might have of intention, Anscombe sounds uncannily like Aquinas when she suggests in §29 that there is a basic distinction often missed in analysis of intentional action, namely that there exists two ways of knowing, and therefore, two objects of knowledge. The first is the non-observational knowledge had by the agent. Anscombe dubs this "knowledge of intentional action." The second is knowledge by observation of what takes place or "knowledge of performance." She continues,

> How can one speak of two different knowledges of exactly the same thing? It is not that there are two descriptions of the same thing, both of which are known, as when one knows that something is red and that it is coloured; no, here the description, opening the window, is identical, whether it is known by observation or by its being one's intentional action. (Ibid. §29)[15]

The problem when one denies this distinction is that intention quickly becomes detached from what happens, "which was also willed in the intention" (Ibid.). Anscombe thinks this is nonsense.

For Anscombe, then, the relationship between these two ways of knowing is something critical. She states bluntly, "I *do* what *happens*. That is to say, when the description of what happens is the very thing which I should say I was doing, then there is no distinction between my doing and the thing's

---

[15]It is reminiscent of Aquinas's dual sense of object in *Summa Theologiae* IaIIae q. 18, a. 6. Here Aquinas states: "Now, in a voluntary action, there is a twofold action, viz. the interior action of the will, and the external action: and each of these actions has its object. The end is properly the object of the interior act of the will: while the object of the external action, is that on which the action is brought to bear." [In actu autem voluntario invenitur duplex actus, scilicet actus interior voluntatis, et actus exterior, et uterque horum actuum habet suum obiectum. Finis autem proprie est obiectum interioris actus voluntarii, id autem circa quod est actio exterior, est obiectum eius.]

happening" (Ibid. – emphasis in original).[16] These two ways of knowing can, in fact, be had by one and the same person, and at times it is quite important that an agent possesses both. Anscombe presents the example of someone writing with his eyes closed. Based on his non-observational knowledge the agent can say what he is writing and it most likely will appear on the paper. However, Anscombe notes, practically speaking the agent's handwriting will likely become quite illegible without the use of his eyes. His external observation of his own intentional act of writing will confirm and assist in that which he intents to write as he goes about performing this act. Anscombe employs this ordinary experience to draw a conclusion between the uses of these two distinct objects of knowing an intentional act.

> ...but isn't the role of all our observation knowledge in knowing what we are doing like the role of the eyes in producing successful writing? That is to say, once given that we have knowledge or opinion about the matter in which we perform intentional actions, our observation is merely an aid, as the eyes are an aid in writing. ... So without the eyes he knows what he writes; but the eyes help to assure him that what he writes actually gets legibly written. (Ibid.)

What Anscombe works out in the passage of the two distinct objects of knowledge concerning intentional actions is rooted in her broader understanding of what intention is. On this account, an agent's intention can be made explicitly manifest in the performance of the action, but there are times in which it does not necessarily appear (Ibid. §25). The idea that there are two distinct objects of knowledge (knowledge of intentional action and knowledge of performance) known in two different

---

[16] I am grateful to Matthew O'Brien for pointing this passage out to me.

ways (by non-observation and by observation) led Anscombe to see intentional action as constituted by the agent's intention, but her notion of intention itself led her to affirm that in some circumstances the agent's intention can be manifest.

What might we do with all of this regarding the intentionalist-physicalist debate in the contemporary Catholic discussion concerning the moral object? Her account of intention and specifically intentional action is a requisite piece to understand her rejection of consequentialism, which refuses to acknowledge the difference between one's intention in acting and one's performance of the same act. The former is understood under one description by the agent (answering the "why" question); the latter can be understood under any description (answering the "what" question) and as such can be open to many and various moral evaluations. Anscombe's positing of intention as a fundamental difference between her absolutism and consequentialism echoes Rhonheimer's own warning that a physicalistic understanding of the moral object has been the conceptual point of departure for proportionalistic understanding of moral action.[17] In this

---

[17]"Traditional physicalism, tending to confuse ontological and moral good – as we still can see in authors like Lawrence Dewan – was not only the point of departure for proportionalism, but is still the rationale of its justification. According to proportionalism, what we – apart from the overall intentions – relate to in choosing this or that action are only things with their 'ontic,' 'physical,' 'pre-moral' value; this theory holds that acts or choices are not able to be morally specified unless one consider all the further intentions with which they are chosen, that is, from what Richard McCormick used to call the 'expanded object.' This is precisely the doctrine rejected by the encyclical *Veritatis splendor* (§79). In fact, I think that proportionalism is precisely an attempt to overcome the problems and inconsistencies of physicalism, the confusion between the moral and the merely ontological; they attempted to do so, not by eliminating what gives rise to these inconsistencies, but by using the very 'physicalist' approach as the foundation for a new theory of moral specification: proportionalism. To consider the morally specifying object as a content of the very action considered as intentional action means to overcome extrinsicism and physicalism, and to provide a basis for overcoming proportionalism" (Rhonheimer, 2011, p. 502).

way, Anscombe understandably becomes the fodder by which
Rhonheimer seeks to return to the perspective of the acting
person.[18]

Nevertheless, as already pointed out, Anscombe's account
of intention also pushes back so as not to shut intention off
from external performance. Crucial to her account in this
regard is her insistence that intention is not merely reducible or
synonymous with mental causality. Indeed, this Anscombean
understanding is waxing among philosophers of intention
contra Donald Davidson. When intention is something more
than mental causality, then it is possible to intimately link it
with performance. Here, performance becomes the source
of knowledge via observation about what an agent intends.
Hence, Anscombe thinks that we are not the sole authorities
over what our intention is (or was). There are checks regarding
one's intention in intentional action and not any answer is
permissible as a sincere response to a "why" question.

In the final analysis, while an Anscombean account of
intention would support the claim that intention is the single
greatest factor constituting the moral object, it would, on one
hand, leave the contemporary Catholic discussion of the role
of the material aspect in the constitution of the moral object
untouched (as this discussion is largely based on a particularly
Thomist approach to the topic). On the other hand, Anscombe's
account of intention would also dictate that an agent could be
wrong about her moral object precisely because she can be
wrong about her intention. This means that even if there were
sudden (and improbable) agreement over the role of material
aspect in constituting or confining the moral object, the
issue of physicalism and intentionalism would continue until
Catholic ethicists had wrestled sufficiently with the very nature
of intention as either merely a mental causality or something
more. Moreover, for those Catholic ethicists who fear that a

---

[18]See footnote 8, above.

misidentification of the role of the material aspect of the moral object would usher in the end of an objective morality, they need not worry that such a misstep would be the final word. There remains the possibility of ample conceptual space for arguing such an objective morality based on the moral object, while still providing ample place for taking into account the perspective of the acting person.

Conclusion

Anscombe is widely acknowledged as coining the phrase "consequentialism" en route to critiquing much of contemporary philosophy as being slave to it. However, surprisingly little attention has been paid to her own alternative: ethical absolutism. Perhaps the wish of contemporary Anglo-analytic virtue ethics to envision its project to be founded upon Anscombe's "Modern Moral Philosophy" has obscured the ultimate foundation of her absolutism. Anscombe does not simply appeal to the virtuous life. Instead, she encourages and performs to an extent the work necessary to return contemporary ethics to the intellectual tools requisite to ultimately make sense of her rejection of consequentialism. Among other things needed for such an account that I have not broached are the distinctions between committed acts and omitted acts, between the voluntary and the intentional, between positive and negative ethical absolutes, and most importantly practical reason's role in these explanations.[19]

---

[19]What Anscombe wrote regarding the absolute norm against murder might serve to illuminate what she thought necessary (though perhaps not an exhaustive list) to reach such a philosophical (re-)establishment of moral absolutism in contemporary philosophical discourse. She writes, "A sufficient consideration of [murder] would comprehend 'the whole man': the agency peculiar to man, his social being and possession of laws, his moral subjectivity and mystical value" (Anscombe, 2005, p. 260). This citation is precisely how Teichmann ends his account of Anscombe's ethical absolutism.

I have argued that when her ethical absolutism is addressed in authors like Teichmann and Richter, it is not presented as it should be. I have offered the distinction between a performance-absolutism and an object-absolutism, arguing that Anscombe's absolutism should be understood in the latter sense. When looking for a tradition from which one might draw the necessary inspiration for such an ethical account, the Catholic intellectual tradition offers one fruitful place of reflection. This seems to have been Anscombe's methodology while working out (some) such issues according to her own insights and philosophical method. In our day the proponents of these two traditions stand to learn something from each other. The aim need not be agreement, but simply mutual benefit. I have tried to indicate in a concrete manner one way in which Anscombe's contribution to the discussion of intention can offer such benefit to the wider Catholic dialogue on the tension between a physicalist and an intentionalist account of the moral object. This same account serves another purpose insofar as it also helps to clarify the kind of ethical absolutist stance Anscombe would have those true to her thought take up and philosophically further. Nevertheless, an account of intention or, even more broadly, the moral object remains only a small, though necessary, contribution to a philosophical account of ethical absolutism.

References

Anscombe, G.E.M., (2000). *Intention*, 2nd ed. Cambridge, MA: Harvard University Press. Originally published 1957.

Anscombe, G.E.M., (2005). Prolegomenon to a Pursuit of the Definition of Murder. *Human Life, Action and Ethics: Essays by G.E.M. Anscombe*, Gormally, L. & Geach, M. (Eds.). Charlottesville, VA.: Imprint Academic, 253-260.

Anscombe, G.E.M., (2005). Modern Moral Philosophy. Cited as in *Human Life, Action and Ethics: Essays by G.E.M.*

Anscombe, Gormally, L. & Geach, M. (Eds.). Charlottesville, VA.: Imprint Academic, 169-195. Originally published in (1958) *Philosophy*, vol. 33, no. 124.

Anscombe, G.E.M., (2008). Twenty Opinions Common among Modern Anglo-American Philosophers. Cited as in *Faith in a Hard Ground: Essays on Religion, Philosophy and Ethics*. Gormally, L. & Geach, M. (Eds.). Charlottesville, VA.: Imprint Academic, 66-68. The essay was originally published in (1987). *Personà, Verità e Morale. Atti del Congresso Internazionale di Teologia Morale*. Roma: Città Nuova Editrice, 49-50.

Aquinas, T., Shapcote, L., Knight, K., Cheung, R., & New Advent, Inc. (1995). *Summa theologica*. Denver, CO: New Advent.

Brock, S. L. (1998). *Action and conduct: Thomas Aquinas and the theory of action*. Edinburgh: T & T Clark.

Brock, S. L., (2008). Veritatis Splendor §78, St. Thomas and (Not Merely) Physical Objects of Moral Acts. *Nova et Vetera, English Edition*, vol. 6, 1-62.

Flannery, K. L. (2003). The Multifarious Moral Object of Thomas Aquinas. *The Thomist* 67, 95-118.

Flannery, K. L. (2007). Moral Taxonomy and Moral Absolutes. *Wisdom's Apprentice: Thomistic Essays in Honor of Lawrence Dewan*. Kwasniewski, P. A. (Ed.). Washington D.C., Catholic University of America Press, 237-256.

Flannery, K. L. (2009). Why does Elizabeth Anscombe Say that We Need Today a Philosophy of Psychology?. *Philosophical Psychology: Psychology, Emotions, and Freedom*. Titus, C. S. (Ed.). Arlington, VA: Institute for the Psychological Sciences Press.

Flannery, K. L. (2013). Thomas Aquinas and the New Natural Law Theory on the Object of the Moral Act. *The National Catholic Bioethics Quarterly*. 13, 79-104.

Geach, M. (2008). Introduction. *Faith in a Hard Ground: Essays on Religion, Philosophy and Ethics*. Geach, M. & Gormally, L. (Eds.). Charlesville, VA: Imprint Academic, xiii- xxvi.

Geach, M. (2011). Introduction. *From Plato to Wittgenstein: Essays by GEM Anscombe*. Exeter, UK: Imprint Academic. Geach, M. & Gormally, L. (Eds.). Charlesville, VA: Imprint Academic, xiii-xx. Catholic Church., & John, P. (1993). *The splendor of truth: Veritatis splendor, encyclical letter*. Boston, Mass: St. Paul Books & Media.

Kaczor, C. (2012). Review of Steven Jensen's Good and Evil Actions: A Journey through Saint Thomas Aquinas. *The Thomist*, 76, 321-324.

Pope John Paul II (1993). *Veritatis Splendor*.

Rhonheimer, M. (2008). *The Perspective of the Acting Person: Essays in the Renewal of Thomistic Moral Philosophy*, Murphy, W. M. (Ed.). Washington, D.C.: Catholic University Press of America.

Rhonheimer, M. (2011). The Moral Object of Human Acts and the Role of Reason According to Aquinas: A Restatement and Defense of My View. *Josephinum Journal of Theology* 18, 454-506.

Richter, D. (2011). *Anscombe's Moral Philosophy*, Lanham, MD: Lexington Books.

Teichmann, R. (2008). *The Philosophy of Elizabeth Anscombe*. New York, NY: Oxford University Press.

Vogler, C. (2013). Aristotle, Aquinas, Anscombe, and the New Virtue Ethic. *Aquinas and the Nicomachean Ethics*, Hoffmann, T., Müller, J., & Perkams, M. (Eds.). New York, NY: Cambridge University Press, 239-258.

Part 3
Anscombe and Double Effect

5. Intended and Unintended Consequences: A Natural Distinction?

Jonathan Buttaci

In his 1952 address to neurologists on the Moral Limits of Medical Research and Treatment, Pope Pius XII declared that "Even the reason for which he acts is neither sufficient nor determining. The patient is bound to the immanent teleology laid down by nature." Pius thus argues that human beings are not entirely free to determine the specification of their actions as good or evil. This may seem to be in conflict with Anscombe's account in *Intention*, in which she focuses on answers to the question 'why' as a way to determine an agent's reasons for acting and by extension his intentional action. On the other hand, Anscombe herself in her 1982 Aquinas Medalist's Address argues that agents are not entirely free to specify their actions by a mere direction of their intention, so to include some effects and exclude others: "Circumstances, and the immediate facts about the means you are choosing to your ends, dictate what descriptions of your intention you must admit." Indeed, some have argued that Anscombe contradicts her earlier *Intention* in making this later point.

In this paper I engage with this question and develop an interpretation of *Intention* which squares with her later claims and with Pius' words. In particular, I examine the famous case of the pumpers Anscombe gives. I ask why, according to Anscombe, the pumper hired before the well has been poisoned can claim not to be intentionally poisoning the inhabitants but merely doing his ordinary job, while the pumper hired after contamination cannot make the same claim. The latter case bears important resemblances to the case of the fat potholer discussed in her Medalist's Address. I argue that what an agent can ordinarily expect to result from his action must figure into our judgment of which effects fall under his intention and which do not: his objective or the means toward it alone are both insufficient to determine this. The decisive difference between the cases is this: the former pumper can appeal to an ordinary course of things where poison does not figure, while the latter pumper cannot. I draw on insights emphasizing the role of the material principle in recent work on Aristotle's natural philosophy to show that matter plays a robust role in hylomorphic physics. I propose that those seeking a broadly hylomorphic account of human action should similarly retain a robust role for the matter of action, following Anscombe in saying "I do what happens."

Three Authorities

My topic is a difficult one about which many people have many divergent opinions. No single paper could give a satisfactory treatment of the entire issue, nor could one engage with every commentator or established opinion. A war rages on, and I come somewhat like a blacksmith who has wandered into a war council with some fine—though indeed not necessarily allied—generals. I know how to make swords and shields, but I am not as familiar with the exact positions of the warring armies over the hill.

Since my primary area of research is ancient philosophy (in particular Aristotle's accounts of nature, soul, intellect, and so on), I am properly two steps removed from most of Anscombe's work in *Intention*, focusing more on the speculative side of philosophy and that *qua* ancient. I hope that I might shed some freshly ancient light on a long-running debate of our own time. My *intention*, at least, is to raise some questions about the way in which nature and the ordinary course of events can constrain the specifications of our actions and what we are responsible for; though what I shall end up *doing* is yet to be seen. But enough with apologies.

In observation of the theme of the volume, I shall begin by quoting something perhaps exclusive to the Catholic intellectual tradition, from Pius XII's address to neurologists on the Moral Limits of Medical Research and Treatment (1952):

> As for the patient, he is not absolute master of himself, of his body or of his soul. He cannot, therefore, freely dispose of himself as he pleases. Even the reason for which he acts is of itself neither sufficient nor determining. The patient is bound to the immanent teleology laid down by nature. (§ 13)[1]

---

[1] Importantly, the sense of "determining" here is formal and not efficient: Pius is not saying that one's reason for acting is not determining of one's action in the sense of one's efficient-causal power or freedom to act. Rather, I take it Pius is saying that one's reason for acting is not determining of how one's action is specified and whether our action under this complete specification counts as good or evil, right or wrong. It is in this latter sense that we are "bound to the immanent teleology laid down by nature." We are of course free to act in the same sense that we are free to sin, but we are not free to determine for ourselves how our action is specified or whether it counts as right or wrong action. The continuation of the quote bears this out: "He has the right of use, limited by

Now the authority with which this statement was given may be disputed (a job for theologians!), and indeed I suspect many Catholic moral philosophers would reject the Pope's claim, or at least a strong reading of it. One might even think that Anscombe's series of 'why' questions as a device to determine intentional action is in tension with the venerable Pope's words: "even the reason for which he acts is of itself neither sufficient nor determining" (ibid.). In this paper, however, I shall outline a program of interpretation according to which Anscombe's theory falls right in line with these words, offering what I take to be friendly clarifications and shifts in emphasis, all with an ancient flavor. In another idiom, I take it both Pius and Anscombe recognize the need for *external constraint* on the content of our intentions; we do not want our reasons for acting to be so untethered to nature and the ordinary course of things that our intentions are left spinning practically frictionless in the void.[2]

Anscombe suggests something along these lines toward the end of her Aquinas Medalist's Address, "Action, Intention and Double Effect" (1982). Instead of Aquinas' treatment of

---

natural finality, of the faculties and powers of his human nature. Because he is a user and not a proprietor, he does not have unlimited power to destroy or mutilate his body and its functions. Nevertheless, by virtue of the principle of totality, by virtue of his right to use the services of his organism as a whole, the patient can allow individual parts to be destroyed or mutilated when and to the extent necessary for the good of his being as a whole. He may do so to ensure his being's existence and to avoid or, naturally, to repair serious and lasting damage which cannot otherwise be avoided or repaired." In short, Pius' denial should be read as normative and not as descriptive: surely, for example, a man has the power to mutilate himself should he so choose. Pius' point is about the goodness and evil of these actions and limitations on man's freedom to determine how his actions are specified. My thanks to John McDowell for suggesting that I clarify this point lest the quote's relevance to the argument of my paper be unclear from the outset.

[2] Cf. John McDowell's (1996) *Mind and World*, especially the fifth lecture wherein he brings his account to bear on practical considerations.

homicidal self-defense, she suggests looking to his treatment of consequences and their bearing on the goodness and badness of an action in order to develop moral principles for these difficult cases:

> If it (the consequent event) is pre-conceived, it manifestly adds to the goodness or badness of the action. For when someone considers that much that is bad can follow from what he does, and does not give it up on that account, this shows that his will is the more inordinate. But if the consequent event is not pre-conceived, then it is necessary to distinguish. For if it follows from that kind of action per se and in most cases, then the consequent event does accordingly add to the goodness or badness of the action; for it is clear that that action is better in kind, from which more goods can follow, and worse, from which more evils are liable to follow. But if it is per accidens, and in rather few cases, then the consequent event does not add to the goodness or to the badness of an action: for there isn't judgment on any matter according to what is per accidens, but only what is per se. (p. 25 n. 5, trans. Anscombe)[3]

Several things should strike us about this passage. First, it seems that the agent is responsible (to some extent)

---

[3]Respondeo dicendum quod eventus sequens aut est praecogitatus, aut non. Si est praecogitatus, manifestum est quod addit ad bonitatem vel malitiam. Cum enim aliquis cogitans quod ex opere suo multa mala possunt sequi, nec propter hoc dimittit, ex hoc apparet voluntas eius esse magis inordinata. Si autem eventus sequens non sit praecogitatus, tunc distinguendum est. Quia si per se **sequitur ex tali actu, et ut in pluribus**, secundum hoc eventus sequens addit ad bonitatem vel malitiam actus, manifestum est enim meliorem actum esse **ex suo genere**, ex quo possunt plura bona sequi; et peiorem, ex quo nata sunt plura mala sequi. Si vero per accidens, et ut in paucioribus, tunc eventus sequens non addit ad bonitatem vel ad malitiam actus, non enim datur iudicium de re aliqua secundum illud quod est per accidens, sed solum secundum illud quod est per se. Quoted in Anscombe (1982) p. 25. Originally from Aquinas' *Summa Theologiae* Ia IIae, q. 20 art. 5 *corpus* (my emphasis added).

for foreseeing the effects of an action, at least according to Aquinas as favorably quoted by Anscombe here. But is it not the point of double effect reasoning, of creating a category of *merely* foreseen effects, precisely in order to avoid this consequence?[4] Furthermore, Aquinas here makes explicit appeal to a distinction between effects which follow regularly and belong to the nature of an action, and those which do not. Even those effects which are not foreseen but follow regularly from an action contribute to that action's goodness or malice.[5] This should strike us as odd, because ignorance is one of the most obvious protests we can make when blamed for some ill happening. Finally, these regular effects seem to bear on the species of the action, and unexpectedly so. We should expect that the means and the end in view should specify the action, but Aquinas is casting the net of action-specification here wider than we might expect. And here, at least, the regular consequences of an action are considered to be per se, and only those effects which follow in few cases are considered to be accidental, at least here. I note this because in other places he insists that neither kind of effect is per se intended.[6]

I shall return to Aquinas' taxonomy of effects later in the paper, but for now I note it because, at the end of her Medalist's Address, Anscombe not only favorably quotes this passage from

---

[4]There may be an important distinction between "praecognitio" and "praescientia." I can only note the possibility here; though I suspect that this distinction may be relevant to my proposed solution, proper consideration of the question must be set aside for another time.

[5]A quote from Aquinas' Commentary on Aristotle's *Physics* is especially relevant: "And I say that this is true if what is outside the intention follows in few cases. For what is always or frequently joined to the effect falls under the intention itself. For it is stupid to say that someone intends something but does not will that which is always or frequently joined to it" (§ 214, p. 110).

[6]Cf. e.g. *de Malo* q. 1, art. 3 ad 15 (Aquinas, 1995, p. 25). The dispute, of course, is how to square what Aquinas says here and what he says in his commentary on the *Physics* regarding the per se object of intention. Happily that issue of interpreting Aquinas, while surely relevant to what I say here, can be set aside for another time.

Aquinas but also develops her own moral principle according to which the natural world gets some grip on the content of our intentions. In Foot's case of the fat potholer caught in the only exit as waters fill the cavern,[7] Anscombe insists that any escape strategy which results immediately in his death would be illicit. Against the protest that one were simply moving an obstruction, not intending to kill him, Anscombe says:

> 'Nonsense,' we want to say, 'doing that is doing this, and so closely that you can't pretend only the first gives you a description under which the act is intentional.' For an act does not merely have many descriptions, under some of which it is indeed not intentional: it has several under which it is intentional. So you cannot choose just one of these, and claim to have excluded others by that. Nor can you simply bring it about that you intend this and not that by an inner act of 'directing your intention.' Circumstances, and the immediate facts about the means you are choosing to your ends, dictate what descriptions of your intention you must admit. (1992, p. 23)

This triptych of quotes from Pius XII, Aquinas and Anscombe, then, forms the basis of my reflection. Worldly facts about which effects follow regularly from our actions, according to these three thinkers, must contribute *somehow* to determining those descriptions of our actions under which they are intentional. But how do we cash this point out in more detail?

Scylla and Charybdis

It is worth noting, in the first place, that there are those who have interpreted Anscombe's words here as in tension or even in contradiction with her theory of intentional action outlined

---

[7] Cf. Philippa Foot's (1967) "The Problem of Abortion and the Doctrine of the Double Effect."

in her earlier *Intention*.[8] These interpretations lean heavily on a point Anscombe makes about a pumper who knowingly but not intentionally pumps poisoned water into a home. Though he is aware of the consequences of his action, Anscombe allows that there are some circumstances under which he can insist that those effects lie outside of his intention (§ 25, pp. 41-45). Those who see a contradiction here with her words above think that her pumper point generalizes to her whole account in *Intention*: the first person has a kind of authority in deciding those descriptions under which his action counts as intentional.

I am generally unconvinced by these interpretations, but I concede to them that the pumper example raises interesting questions—a rather uncontroversial concession, I admit. I shall return to the pumper example in detail later on, but I first make a general remark about this debate now in order to frame the paper: I take it Anscombe is trying to plot a middle course between two extremes, both in *Intention* and in her Medalist's Address. On the one hand, already in *Intention* she clearly disagrees with those who would make the content of one's intentions an entirely private matter which is fully determinable by the agent's objective, thereby giving the agent a kind of first-personal trump-card, saying:

> And against the background of the qualifications we have introduced, we can epitomize the point by saying 'Roughly speaking, a man intends to do what he does.' But of course that is *very* roughly speaking. It is right to formulate it, however, as an antidote against the absurd thesis which is sometimes maintained: that a man's intended action is only described by describing his *objective*. (§ 25, p. 45)

---

[8]Cf. e.g. John Finnis' (2011b) "Intention and Side Effects," republished in *Intention and Identity: Collected Essays Volume II*. See also Finnis' (2011a) "Anscombe on Spirit and Intention," republished in *Intention and Identity: Collected Essays Volume II*.

On the other hand, Anscombe wants to insist that not every consequence of one's actions (and, perhaps more importantly, one's failures to act) falls under the agent's intention or figures into a description of his action under which it is intentional. Her reasons for this become obvious when considering hard moral cases where one must choose between committing an evil action (e.g. killing an innocent) and suffering still greater evils (e.g. several others being murdered by one's deranged captor should you fail to murder). In the case, one's abstaining from murdering one does not constitute murdering the several others, or in general that one's abstaining from φ-ing does not constitute intending all of the consequences of not φ-ing.[9] Thus, I take it, Anscombe is searching for a middle way where not all of the consequences of one's (in)action are intended, but where the content of one's intentions are not entirely up to one and, as it were, in the head.

This present paper, then, is not meant principally as a response to those who take either of these extremes; plenty has been written in reply and I shall assume for the present discussion that neither extreme is a plausible view, at least as a matter of interpreting Anscombe. My paper is more directly an engagement with those who agree that neither horn of the dilemma will do and are looking to further explain and specify Anscombe's safe passage through the physicalist's Scylla and the first-personalist's Charybdis.

An Itch and a Bell

I want to raise a series of questions building upon some of the examples Anscombe introduces in order to zero in on this

---

[9] I take it that the distinction between action and omission here is not relevant; one's not φ-ing implies taking other actions (e.g. setting down the revolver), so that the consequences of not φ-ing may be the same as the consequences of ψ-ing, where to ψ is to do take those positive actions that are implied in not φ-ing. It would be absurd if the source of moral absolution were the omission, since on such an account the agent would remain responsible for the ill effects *qua* consequences of ψ-ing.

impingement of nature on spirit. Early in her discussion of practical knowledge, she briefly mentions an example of a man who is unknowingly ringing a bell. She gives this as a case of someone who lacks practical knowledge in this very respect – "Why are you ringing that bell?" He replies, "Good heavens! I didn't know *I* was ringing it!" (§ 28, p. 51).

Of course the person doing the ringing knew *that* the bell was ringing: he knew what was happening but not that *he was doing it.* I find this to be a particularly interesting example, because once the agent discovers that he was the one ringing the bell (by perhaps leaning against a button), he can no longer reject the question, "Why are you ringing the bell?" Once he knows that "doing that is doing this," he can no longer claim that he was not intentionally ringing the bell that he had been ringing if he were to go on ringing it by (e.g.) continuing to lean against the button. This seems to be Anscombe's view, since it is practical knowledge itself which he previously lacked, but now has.

Let us develop the example some to capture the point. Suppose someone has an itch on his back as he stands, say, waiting for his take-out food. Caught in the grips of the itch, he leans back against the wall and discovers there is a little bump there, just rough enough and at the right height to do the trick. After relieving the horrible itch he realizes that a bell has been going off for some time, though he is unsure when it started. His fellow patrons are looking at him, presumably because he scratched more vigorously than appropriate. Trying to divert the attention from his embarrassing scratching to the restaurant's annoying noises, he asks, "That bell sure is annoying, eh?" One gruff patron responds, "Yeah, so why were you ringing it? The button is on the wall behind you!" We can imagine the man's eager apology in this moment, protesting that he had no idea that he was the one ringing the bell, since he had been caught up with scratching the itch. It is clear that in this first case, ignorance is the reason the bell ringing counts as an unintended effect.

A few minutes pass and the bell starts ringing again. It stops as soon as it starts, and immediately the man swears up and down, apologizing, saying that he lost his balance or perhaps momentarily forgot that the button was right behind him. In this case, forgetfulness or an involuntary bodily movement is the cause of his ability to reject our special sense of the question 'why.' I take it most every view is agreed on these initial cases of ignorance, forgetfulness, and involuntary bodily movement.

A few more minutes pass and the bell starts ringing again. But instead of stopping immediately, the ringing continues until people begin to yell at the man, who is now vigorously scratching his back on the button. "I'm sorry, I know that I'm making the bell ring but this itch is unbearable!" How do we carve up this action? The man's stated end, and I think we can take him at his word, is to scratch an itch. His means are to use a semi-sharp nub on the wall which he later discovers to be a button connected to a bell. It seems to me that we want to say that he intentionally rings the bell, but the effect seems to fall outside of a straightforward specification of the end and means. To motivate this point more exactly, we might even imagine it to be the metal ring *around* the button which is doing the scratching, not the button itself—that the button is depressed is perhaps a necessary consequence of his using the metal ring around the button, but the button itself being pressed down does not figure in the scratching. So, the bell's ringing does not, after all, form an essential part of the scratching.

Let us alter the example still more to draw out this accidental relationship between scratching and ringing. Perhaps this man has a habit of scratching his back on this very button casing while waiting for his take out—a very strange man, indeed!—but only very recently has the owner activated the bell to which it is connected. Does it make any difference to our case when the man ordinarily can scratch his back (and has many times, perhaps over several years) *without* ringing a bell? When the patrons yell at him in *this* case, can our itchy patron not blame the owner for the noise? After all, he is just behaving as he always has; it is the owner who has changed things. In contrast, when in the former case the patron persists in his scratching despite the ringing, he cannot excuse himself by saying, "The ringing does not figure into the specification of the means I adopt in scratching my back; the ringing is a causally necessary effect that I nevertheless do not intend!" "Nonsense!" we want to say, because "doing that is doing this," at least in the ordinary case. But again, perhaps things are different when the man is in the habit of scratching on the button casing without the bell ever ringing.

In order to save both of these intuitions, I think what the agent can ordinarily expect to result from his action must be taken into account. I now turn to a more developed example from *Intention* to show that Anscombe would agree on this point.

Three Pumpers

Anscombe famously introduces the example of three pumpers (in my reckoning) who pump water to a house from a well which has been tainted by the gradual laying of a cumulative poison (some may take issue with my numbering, but that is a minor point which will soon become clear). The first of these pumpers has been on the job for a while and has been informed that the well has been poisoned.[10] He does not particularly like the inhabitants or their political program, and so his usual job of pumping is now directed toward a further

---

[10]We may even imagine a fourth (or perhaps more properly, a zero-th) pumper who is completely ignorant of the well having been poisoned and performs his job as usual. He would (and I take it all the accounts in the vicinity here agree) be unintentionally poisoning the inhabitants.

revolutionary end. The second pumper (or the first pumper considered in a second variation) has similarly been pumping water on this estate for a while and has been informed of the poison, but he does not care one bit about the political world around him. When asked why he is poisoning the inhabitants he neither claims ignorance nor confesses an intention to polish them off, but rather insists that he neither cares nor wants any trouble and is simply doing his job. The third pumper, whom Anscombe mentions very briefly, is one who, upon being hired, was told that the well was tainted.

It seems that for Anscombe the first pumper both intends and is responsible for the deaths, the second pumper does not intend (but is plausibly still responsible for)[11] the deaths, and the third pumper both intends and is responsible for the deaths. Importantly, the difference between these three men does not seem to be their responsibility for the deaths, but rather whether the description of their action "poisoning the inhabitants" counts as intentional. And on this count, unlike the second pumper, the third pumper cannot (on Anscombe's view) protest that he is simply doing his job. She argues that the pumping of poisoned water is part of the specification of the means the third pumper adopts in order to earn his pay (§ 25, p. 44). As a result he is not free to protest that he is just doing his job when he pumps poisoned water, while whether the deaths of the inhabitants count as intended effects of "doing my job" remains an open question for the first two pumpers. This raises important questions about when it is available to an agent to reject a 'why' question, and when a questioner can call him on his 'nonsense.'

---

[11] "The question arises: what can be the interest of the intention of the man we have described, who was only doing his usual job etc.? It is certainly not an ethical or legal interest; if what he said was true, *that* will not absolve him from guilt of murder!" (§ 25, p. 45).

Anscombe gestures toward at least two related answers, as far as I can tell. The first is her discussion in *Intention* about this third pumper who, upon being hired, is told about the poison. She regards the pumping of poisoned water, resulting in the death of the inhabitants, to figure into the *means by which* the third pumper earns his pay, and therefore he cannot protest that he only wanted to earn his pay, rejecting the question as to why he poisoned the inhabitants. She gives a similar answer in her Medalist's Address, arguing that when the ill effect is *immediate*, such as the boulder crushing the stuck potholer, then it falls under the means by which the agent acts. Broadly speaking, then, we can object to an agent's dissociating themselves from some ill effect by insisting that it falls under the means with which the agent's professed end is achieved.

I am not sure this is enough to do the trick, however; that is, I am uncertain this is enough to say in justifying (and winning!) an argument with the agent. In each case we can easily imagine him insisting, "No, I'm just moving this rock to escape; its falling on Joe is not a part of my means-end reasoning," or "No, I'm just pumping for pay; its poisoning the inhabitants is not part of my means-end reasoning," or "No, I'm just scratching my back on this sharp button casing; the bell's ringing is not a part of my means-end reasoning." The agent in each case has a plausible re-description of the means in which the ill effect does not figure. Indeed, if in some nearby possible world the ill effect were not to follow from his adopted means, the agent would do nothing further to achieve that effect: he genuinely does not want the ill effect to happen. Immediacy is a more plausible alternative, but that approach also could admit of serious disagreement. How can we settle these disputes or even defend our challenging (e.g.) the third pumper at all, especially when we were *right* to grant the second pumper a first-personal authority? Or put differently, what is the difference between the second and third pumpers in virtue of which poisoning the inhabitants must count as intentional for one but not the other?

A Preliminary Conclusion

While I agree with some critics of Anscombe that linguistic convention and immediacy of result simply will not do here,[12] I disagree with them and concur in her final judgment about these cases. And the idea that our first-personal plan provides a form to some of the things that happen but not to others is a promising way to go, and yet this must be spelled out in more detail as to which happenings fall under that form and which are potentially excluded from it. Hylomorphism, in other words, seems to be the very middle course we were seeking, but this is not yet stated in determinate enough terms to decide our cases.[13]

---

[12]Again, see Finnis' (2011b) "Intention and Side Effects," republished in *Intention and Identity: Collected Essays Volume II*: "I think this attempt to distinguish the intended from the unintended by reference to sheer physical 'immediacy' of cause and effect is unsound, a confusion of categories, an elision of human behaviour with human action. I know of no *argument* that Anscombe has brought against her own analysis, twenty-five years earlier in her book *Intention*, of the intentions of the man who pumps poisoned water into a house. In one variant of the situation, 'the man's intention might not be to poison [the inhabitants] but only to earn his pay' by doing his usual job" (p. 192).

[13]A paper on this topic with which I am in general agreement is (O'Brien & Koons, 2012). My paper takes a slightly different angle, but only topically, by considering the supposed tension between the case of Anscombe's pumpers and her judgment of the potholer case in her Medalist's Address. As we shall see, I also draw more explicitly on recent work in Aristotle's natural philosophy. While I am generally in agreement that many accounts err in positing an intention/behavior dualism which is opposed to a more hylomorphic model of human action, I am more concerned with those views that claim to be hylomorphic but still underappreciate the role of the material principle as applied to the practical case, i.e. the 'what happens' part of 'I do what happens.'

My suggestion is that our dependence on first personal reasoning to decide the case between the first and second pumper is the exception, not the rule. This is supported by the idea that, according to Anscombe, *in general* we should look to what the agent actually does to determine what he intends. Indeed, let us recall that she proposes this precisely as an antidote to the "absurd thesis" limiting intended action to an agent's first-personal objective (§ 25, p. 45). If I am right, then those who accused Anscombe of disavowing her *Intention* in her Medalist's Address were wrong to generalize from the exceptional case of the second pumper.

One significant difference, and perhaps the *decisive* difference, between the first two pumpers and the third is that in the former case there is an "ordinary course of things" apart from the pumping of poisoned water to which the first two pumpers can appeal. The poison is introduced into this ordinary scheme and creates a deviant result: now instead of simply providing water to the inhabitants their ordinary job results in providing *poisoned* water to them.[14] This effect falls out of what is ordinary for them. In the case of the revolutionary first pumper, we might say that the effect is *extraordinary*, insofar as his intention changes in view of this further end now available to him. The apolitical second pumper, however, is able to foresee with certainty this *unordinary* result while maintaining that it falls outside of his intention to do his job *as usual*. In the third case the pumping of poisoned water is inseparable precisely because there is no "ordinary course of

---

[14]Matthew O'Brien has suggested to me that there may be something wrong with how Anscombe describes the case, since initially the pumper is described as "pumping water into the cistern which supplies the drinking water of the house" (§ 23, p. 37). That the water is no longer potable once poisoned, he suggests, raises difficulties for the case. For the present I note the interesting issue in order to set it aside, assuming here a simpler extensional reading of "drinking water."

things" apart from which the poisoning stands: for the third pumper, the pumping of poisoned water *just is* the ordinary result of doing his job. Thus specifying the means of doing his job *in his case* must include the pumping of poisoned water.

So, the only relevant difference between the first two pumpers and the third pumper is their (in)ability to appeal to an "ordinary course of things," so that this difference must ground Anscombe's different judgments in each case. It is because the poisoning deviates from the "ordinary course of things" that the second pumper can honestly claim that the effects of the poison are not intended, whereas when the third pumper makes the same protest we say instead, "No, doing that is doing this, at least in *your* case." Anscombe's answer already presupposes this fact about the ordinary course of things. This leads me to the following conclusion: in *ordinary* circumstances, all truly foreseen effects of our actions fall under our intention even if they are not the aim itself we are trying to achieve. It is only in the case of foreseen effects which fall *outside* of this ordinary course of things that they can in some cases also fall outside of our intention despite their being foreseen.[15]

This principle, as Anscombe might say, covers a great many cases and I think avoids the sorts of problems we have come to expect when the discussion comes down to immediacy, directedness, or closeness of these effects. It explains, in particular, the rulings Anscombe hands down in the pumper and potholer cases, and further can speak to the standard cases to be distinguished by double effect reasoning, without losing her insight about the *second* pumper. The public grounds

---

[15]I say "can in some cases" because, of course, someone can reason, as it were, 'on the fly' about unordinary effects and intend that they come about, as in the case of the revolutionary first pumper. But that a difference in intention is even possible between the first and second pumper is a result of the irregularity of that effect.

upon which we can challenge the pumpers and to which they can appeal is the ordinariness of the effect in question.

I have so far spoken of *ordinariness* as opposed to what effects are *natural* in order to capture the artificial cases like bell ringing and poison pumping. While I do not mean to deny that in many cases the ordinary course of things is going to be defined by nature herself (indeed, this has perhaps been my line all along), to make appeal to nature and naturalness of an effect still leaves many cases obscure, particularly those cases that involve human contrivance. While I grant its immense importance, natural teleology cannot explain the difference between pumpers two and three, since someone may argue that pumping poisoned water is unnatural and irregular even for the third pumper. So to avoid one kind of obscurity in these cases I have leaned heavily on another obscure but nevertheless intuitive notion of the ordinary course of things, what a typical agent can ordinarily expect to happen as a result of a certain kind of action, whether this ordinary course be purely natural or contain an admixture of art.

What's the Matter?

Some want to make a strong distinction between the intended means and all of the causally necessary effects of our actions (which are sometimes foreseen). After all, Anscombe herself defends her judgment against the agent's protests in both cases by saying that he cannot not will the means, though I find this move incomplete as I have said. One may worry that on my account by replacing the distinction between intended means and causally necessary effects with the distinction between two sorts of effects (ordinary and unordinary), that too many effects will come out as intentional because in our modern scientific worldview every truly foreseen effect will count as a causally necessary effect. Ultimately, the worry goes, no effect is truly unordinary since every effect – even defective – comes by cause. This is especially true, the worry continues, should an effect be foreseen or foreseeable. As a result, one might think that I have veered too far in the direction of the physicalist's Scylla in avoiding the first-personalist's Charybdis.

My reply would be to dispute what counts as causally necessary, or perhaps to concede the breadth of that category and argue that the *ordinary* effects are only one subclass of it. This raises an important point about what assumptions about nature we wheel in when discussing action and intention. One way of motivating the foreseen/intended distinction is to argue that if we were not able to draw the distinction, then rational agents would be as bombs going off, setting off infinite chains of changes in the world which they intended or for which they were responsible. We might imagine the argument setting up a kind of dilemma: agents cause infinitely many infinite causal chains of physical happenings, and without a meaningful foreseen/intended distinction they will turn out to be responsible for either all or none of these effects. In short, without a meaningful foreseen/intended distinction, we are without principled means of distinguishing between different consequences and thereby avoiding the dilemma. Amid the chaos of worldly happenings, then, we can find solace in 'why' questions as a device to sort it all out.[16]

Importantly, however, this line of reasoning already makes an assumption about the character of the natural world. In an effort, perhaps, to avoid having to speak to the realm of law and of the empirically falsifiable, many philosophers take refuge in a moral device *alone* to draw the line in every case. While I do not deny that there are cases in which the line is finally determined by the agent's reasons for acting (such as between the first two pumpers), I want also to affirm that there are cases in which the ordinary course of things and

---

[16] This style of argument was suggested to me by Candace Vogler in conversation.

nature herself imposes conditions on the agent's intention in the shape of "doing that *just is* doing this" (such as with the third pumper and the drowning spelunkers).

An *exclusive* use of a moral device and appeal to an agent's own reasons for acting, then, relies upon an assumption about the world, namely that there is no principled way to distinguish between happenings in the world *except* by the practical reasoning of rational agents. Every effect which is causally necessitated is on a par antecedent to an agent's reasoning, and the notion of "causal necessity" is one taken in a broad way from modern philosophy. As a student of ancient philosophy, I am surprised that this should be assumed by some who take themselves to be modern-day allies of Aristotle in the realm of practical philosophy. It is surely the case that the many happenings of the natural world can appear to be chaotic, particularly given a certain conception of nature common today. But I take it that Aristotle's single greatest insight, from which all of his other insights flow, is to resist the charm of this appearance by offering a principled middle way between Heraclitus and Parmenides in accounting for worldly change. I take it this middle way provides a natural philosophical model for avoiding the Agents-as-Bombs dilemma above.

Heraclitus, as caricatured by Aristotle, stood for the idea that change is both inevitable and unintelligible, that no one happening or change or attribute is ontologically privileged. Parmenides, again as caricatured, held that change was impossible and therefore trivially unintelligible.[17] Aristotle's synthesis as a matter of *natural* philosophy was to insist that in the world there are those changes which proceed according to a nature or form and are therefore intelligible and those changes which are not so governed or otherwise deviate in some way, about which Heraclitus might have been correct in some very limited way. In fact, one cannot understand the true

---

[17] Cf. e.g. *de Caelo* III.1 298b12-34.

upshot of hylomorphism except against the background of this debate.[18] After all, it is because of his (supposed) commitment to Heraclitean flux in the sensible world that Aristotle thought Plato had to posit a separate intelligible world of eternal Forms.[19] Aristotle's version of hylomorphism, at any rate, is proposed as an alternative to a Platonic view of form yoked to a Heraclitean view of matter.

And so, as a student of Aristotle I am not convinced that moral philosophy can be conducted while taking a neutral position on this question in natural philosophy: as soon as one claims to be neutral one has already made an assumption in favor of the Heraclitean flux and is liable to conclude that worldly happenings are only intelligible insofar as form is imposed upon them from the outside, perhaps in our case in the form of an agent's intention. In contrast, one might suppose (with Aristotle) that the world is already formed, by nature and still further by art, and that our intentions serve as the form of things already formed. Insofar as this is so, we can distinguish between those happenings which are formally inseparable and those which are separable, conceived

---

[18] Cf. *Physics* I, in which Aristotle develops his matter/form/privation distinction as a partial reply to Heraclitean and Parmenidean accounts alike.

[19] Cf. *Metaphysics* A.6 987a29-b10: "After the systems we have named came the philosophy of Plato, which in most respects followed these thinkers, but had peculiarities that distinguished it from the philosophy of the Italians. For, having in his youth first become familiar with Cratylus and with the Heraclitean doctrines (that all sensible things are ever in a state of flux and there is no knowledge about them), these views he held even in later years. Socrates, however, was busying himself about ethical matters and neglecting the world of nature as a whole but seeking the universal in these ethical matters, and fixed thought for the first time on definitions; Plato accepted his teaching, but held that the problem applied not to any sensible thing but to entities of another kind—for this reason, that the common definition could not be a definition of any sensible thing, as they were always changing. Things of this other sort, then, he called Ideas, and sensible things, he said, were apart from these, and were all called after these; for the multitude of things which have the same name as the Form exist by participation in it."

antecedently to the imposition of our intention. And if this is true, then it is precisely because we are not simply like bombs going off, *nor is anything else in nature either*, that we can make the foreseen/intended distinction at all. My distinction between ordinary and unordinary effects, far from rivaling the foreseen/intended distinction, in fact grounds its very intelligibility.

Of course in insisting that these sorts of effects are intended I am not arguing that every one of them must be the agent's aim, either proximate or remote. I grant that there is a sense of "intended" which is only properly said of one's objective, so that many intended effects (in my sense) would be things the agent would not repeat if by some fluke they failed to obtain. In this sense I do not take myself to be denying the standard view which leans heavily on a means-end analysis for what counts as intended, but rather I take myself to be enriching and more completely explicating it. Recalling the passage in Aquinas on consequences, he speaks there as if the regular effects of an action are a per se part of the nature of the action itself, while irregular effects are accidental. In other texts, however, he speaks of all consequences as accidental and neither as per se intended, though context suggests that he may mean something more restricted in those passages.[20] The question arises: which sense of per se and which sense of accidental is most relevant *here*?

I would argue that it depends a great deal on the context. But if we consider the notion of per se accidents from Aristotelian logic and natural philosophy, the general idea is that these are features which belong to a thing in virtue of the kind of thing that it is, while nevertheless not figuring in the essential definition of that thing.[21] The classic example is risibility, or the sense of humor proper to man. This follows from the

---

[20]See again *de Malo* q. 1, art. 3 ad 15 (Aquinas, 1995, p. 25).
[21]Cf. *Posterior Analytics* I.4 73a35-b24; *Topics* I.5 102a18-31, V.5 134a5-135b7.

essence of man and belongs to him per se, but is nevertheless not his essence. We might say that various physiological facts also belong to this category of per se accidents. My proposal would be to allow the notion of per se accidents to more richly inform its place in action theory, so that the death of the inhabitants for the third pumper and the death of the fat spelunker for his companions both belong to this category since, for them, these effects follow from the ordinary course of things given the action they take.

This raises a question about counterfactual reasoning and in what sense it figures in this kind of practical reasoning and judgment. On one view of intentional action, one which can surely claim to be a version of hylomorphism, only those worldly happenings which essentially (or non-accidentally) constitute the means adopted or the end sought count as truly intentional. On this view, we can make use of counterfactuals in order to decide the case: "Would the agent still perform some part of the action with an ill effect if she could achieve her end without doing it?" If the answer is "no" then this does not belong essentially to the action. Or similarly: "Would the agent repeat the action if the foreseen ill effect were to fail to obtain?"

It is not clear to me that this kind of reasoning is sufficient, either on its own or as an explication of the moral judgments Anscombe has handed down. After all, the drowning potholers would not otherwise kill their obese companion, nor would they toss another boulder his way if the first one should fail to polish him off. This counterfactual test is insufficient, therefore, to explain her judgment in that case. Nor again is it sufficient in the case of the third pumper. Suppose the third pumper is hired with the knowledge that the well is contaminated but by some fluke the inhabitants survive the poison. He just wants to earn his pay like pumper number two—by stipulation we can take him at his word—and yet Anscombe disallows even this much, arguing that from the beginning the third pumper, in accepting the job as described, must intentionally pump *poisoned* water. According to her, the third pumper's only excuse would be if he made a genuine attempt to cheat the one who hired him. But if the poisoning failed to obtain for some other reason outside of his control, such as some rare immunity to the poison in question, the third pumper would not take other action to kill the inhabitants. After all, he just wants to earn his pay.

On my view there is a rather different form of counterfactual analysis appropriate to the case, and it concerns the separability of effects in the ordinary course of things. The focus of the former style of reasoning is the deliberation and agency of some agent; the focus of mine is the world itself. Here we place the counterfactual reasoning in the voice of our agent as a kind of excuse: "If only the restaurant owner hadn't connected the bell..." or "If only this revolutionary hadn't contaminated the well with poison..." In these cases the counterfactual points to a state of affairs unaffected by some natural deviation or artificial intervention which, at some time in the agent's history, was the case. That is, while presently counterfactual, these cases point to an actual state of affairs in the past. When an agent (or his judge) engages in my sort of counterfactual reasoning, he considers a state of affairs that was the ordinary or default case of his action, showing how the ill effect has resulted by some chance or blameworthy intervention by another, some deviation from what ordinarily happens. I suggest that this version of counterfactual reasoning, as opposed to the kind previously described, goes much further to explaining Anscombe's judgment in the case of the fat potholer and the third pumper.

Some Difficult Cases

My suggestion, I think, justifies the intuitive answers to standard cases. But someone may object with the following examples.[22] First, someone proposes to build highways in an undeveloped part of the world. He knows that some people who use the highways will eventually die in car accidents. But on the standard view, this foreseen effect is not willed because it does not figure into a straightforward specification of the means or the end of the action. My view, my opponent argues, commits me to saying that people who build roads intend the deaths, since always or for the most part some people who use the roads will die.

The building of roads, to be sure, almost certainly results in the death of an occasional motorist. My reply is that it matters where the "always or for the most part" operator figures into our specification of this effect. Surely always or for the most part motorists occasionally die, but it does not follow that always or for the most part motorists die *simpliciter*. Considered simply, people die only *rarely* as a result of motor accidents and therefore as a result of building roads; indeed, as the objector herself argues, we call such happenings *accidents*. Always or for the most part humans are occasionally born with congenital defects, but that is not the proper way to use the operator "always or for the most part." For this reason I am not convinced my account differs from the standard account in this case, because I differ from that model only in cases where the effect follows ordinarily from the action taken. Motorist deaths do *not* result ordinarily or for the most part from the building of roads. On the other hand, if some public works project made it so that users always or for the most part died, and foreseeably so, we *do* want to say that the deaths are intended even if those implementing the project were to regret the deaths very much or if they should permit

---

[22]I am grateful to Candace Vogler, Jennifer Frey, and John O'Callaghan for suggesting these three cases to me as problems for my account when I presented a related paper at the 3rd Annual Thomas Aquinas Workshop at Mount Saint Mary College in Newburgh, NY. Vogler (2013) also mentions some of these examples in her address at the American Catholic Philosophical Association.

the occasional survivor to go on living. In that case, I rather worry that it is my objector, and not I, who is hard pressed to save our ordinary moral intuitions about those ill effects counting as intentional.

Second case: St. Thomas More defends the church's teaching on marriage against King Henry's divorce. In so doing he foresees that he will be imprisoned and perhaps even martyred, thereby abandoning his wife and children (who were mostly grown at the time, but putting that aside). On the standard view the abandonment of family is a foreseen but unintended effect because it does not figure in the end or the means of defending church teaching or of failing to assent to heresy. An objector might say that according to my view the abandonment of his children comes out as an intended effect. But importantly here St. Thomas can protest (like the second pumper) that he was just doing what he had ordinarily done for years in service to the king. Thus on my view, the abandonment of his family is foreseen but need not be intended precisely because it deviates from what the agent has ordinarily come to expect; indeed, it was due principally to Thomas More that the English Sovereign was named a Defender of the Faith. Contrast this with the case of a missionary to hostile lands and peoples, or perhaps a Christian who served in the court (or cabinet) of an avowed enemy of the Church: in these cases the agent cannot ordinarily expect to defend the faith in his public role without suffering violence.

Final case: when I walk to school the rubber inevitably wears down on my shoes. On my view, it looks like this comes out as an intended effect since it follows regularly and is an ordinarily foreseeable effect of my walking, though we often do not think of it. But this seems strange to the average ear: surely we do not see to it that our shoes wear down and we would not repeat our walk if they should fail to wear down the appropriate (though almost negligible) amount.

So even if I am aware of the rubber wearing down as I walk, what could it mean to say that I intend it? Two points are relevant here. First, as Michael Thompson (2008) notes, one need not have an occurrent thought of something for it to belong to one's intention, supposing one is generally not ignorant of it (p. 108). It need not occur to me or be an act of explicit calculation to figure into a description of my action *as* intentional.

Secondly, this case is weird because we do not typically have a moral norm praising or prohibiting the wearing down of one's shoes. The case becomes much less strange if we suppose that a mother tell her son not to wear out his nice school shoes. If he chooses to walk home in them instead of taking the bus, given that he generally understands how shoes wear out through use, he cannot protest to his mother that he only intended to walk home on a nice spring day, merely foreseeing and tolerating *but not intending* the wear on the shoes. "I regret it very much, and would not have otherwise worn the rubber down if I could have avoided it!" he pleads. But on my view of this case, the moral norm elucidates and makes salient something which was already implicit in the agent's intentional action. The ordinariness of this effect was already there, so that it has been a potentially intended effect all along. The moral norm introduced by the boy's mother, on my view, renders explicit and actualizes the rubber-wearing-down as an intended consequence which was already potentially present within the action. But I would not go so far as to say that the wearing down of his shoes was not intentional prior to his mother's issuing the command.[23]

---

[23]My thanks to John O'Callaghan for prompting me to explain the relevance of a moral norm. I believe my view still differs from his own, but his suggestions have prompted me to introduce the language of potentiality and actuality here, as a way to make sense of the practical salience of some effect antecedent and consequent to the establishment of a moral norm concerning it.

A Final Objection

As suggested earlier, someone might object to my account in general charging, *incidit in scyllam cupiens vitare charybdim*, so that in claiming that the regular effects of my actions fall under my intention, I have simply taken the physicalist horn of the dilemma with which we began.[24] Although I rightly oppose those who have over-emphasized the place of the *form* of our intention to the exclusion of what actually happens, the objector argues, I also go too far but in the other direction, over-emphasizing the role of *material* happenings in action specification. To this I reply with the words of Aristotle, though he gave them in a different context: "That is why we can dismiss as unnecessary the question whether the soul and the body are one: it is as though we were to ask whether the wax and its shape are one, *or generally the matter of a thing and that of which it is the matter*" (De Anima II.1 412b5-8; emphasis mine).[25] It is this last line that I find very interesting for our purposes because it suggests that it is hard, and perhaps even wrongheaded, to distinguish too strongly the matter of something from the matter-form composite itself. Matter itself, when formed, is what constitutes the composite; this is precisely why Anscombe's slogan "I do what happens" is so brilliant. Indeed, a hand is only homonymously a hand when separated from the body, and so it is difficult or perhaps even wrongheaded to specify the matter independently of a specification of the composite of which it is the matter.[26]

Indeed, recent work focusing on Aristotle's biological works bear out the point: contrary to what we typically mean by "essentialism," the substantial form does not give

---

[24]Again, this is the shape of a general objection raised by Jennifer Frey to an earlier presentation of this paper.

[25]See also *Metaphysics* H.6 1045a7-b7.

[26]Cf. *de Anima* II.1 412b10-413a3.

form to undifferentiated prime matter.[27] Instead the form is an active principle which forms matter, while matter as a passive principle can place serious limits on what form it can admit. This is perhaps why per se accidents are so important in specifying and learning about substances, because they belong in many cases to the proximate material principles themselves. In addition, family resemblance and heritability of traits are due to material principles in Aristotle's biology. And finally, many attributes of animals are explained in material terms; for example, horned animals lose a row of teeth due to defect of earthy material.[28]

How is this relevant? Well, it seems obvious to me how one could go wrong in trying to specify the form apart from the matter in the natural case, by understanding the soul to be wholly unrelated and even unspecified by the material in which it inheres; for example, a horse-soul in a man's body or vice-versa. But how could it go wrong the other way, trying to specify the matter apart from the form? Given a certain background view of nature and of material principles, namely one that rejects both Heraclitus and Parmenides in favor of a hylomorphic middle ground, the very attempt to specify some matter is to say *what form it bears*. In doing so, one can privilege aspects of the material organization over others, pointing to the definitive and even definitional importance of one thing over another. But in specifying what some stuff is, one comes across ways in which the matter is constituted which must be admitted as necessary and proper to the whole composite, while nevertheless not absolutely essential to the definition of what the composite is.

---

[27]See for example Kelsey (2010), Frey (2007), Lennox (2001), and Balme (1987).
[28]Cf. *Parts of Animals* III.2 663b36-334a2.

Many people in a certain school of action theory seem to want to have a hylomorphic model, just as those who interpret Aristotle generally want a hylomorphic natural philosophy. But it seems to me that one can easily misunderstand Aristotle as privileging form more than he actually does by underappreciating his analysis of material principles in the biological works. So too we risk underemphasizing the material principle in our analysis of intentional action. We should not forget that Anscombe herself gave the matter of intentional action a certain dignity when she declared that "I do what happens" (§ 29, pp. 52-53).

Coda: Intention and Moral Responsibility

I should like to end by reconsidering Aquinas' taxonomy of effects which I cited at the beginning of the paper. His taxonomy, I take it, is given in reference to our general responsibility for effects as agents, not whether they count as intentional. This is why for Aquinas, in the passage quoted by Anscombe, any foreseen ill effect will count against the agent and so the distinction between foreseen and unforeseen is treated as more fundamental.

Fig. 1 : Aquinas' Taxonomy (focus on responsibility)

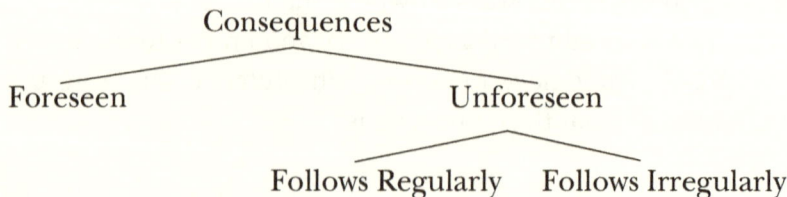

Consequences

Foreseen   Unforeseen

Follows Regularly   Follows Irregularly

I think, however, that this is compatible with a view that focuses alternatively on the agent's intention. On my view, as regards this question, the more fundamental distinction is between regular/natural/per se effects and those that follow irregularly or accidentally. Among effects which follow "outside of the ordinary course of events," there are those that are unforeseen and those that are foreseen. Obviously we are neither responsible for nor do we intend unforeseen and irregular effects of our actions. But when it comes to the foreseen irregular effects, we must draw a distinction. As with the second and third pumpers, both will be responsible for poisoning the inhabitants. But the second pumper, insofar as he can and does appeal to what he does in the ordinary course of things, disavowing any further revolutionary intent, does not intend this foreseen ill effect. On the contrary, the third pumper cannot make such an appeal, since there is no "ordinary course of events" to which he can point, and therefore no gap between "just doing my job" and "poisoning the inhabitants." Thus, from the perspective of intention, this revised taxonomy helps capture the same result though allows for more precise differentiation between cases.

Fig. 2 : My Alternative Taxonomy (focus on intentionality)

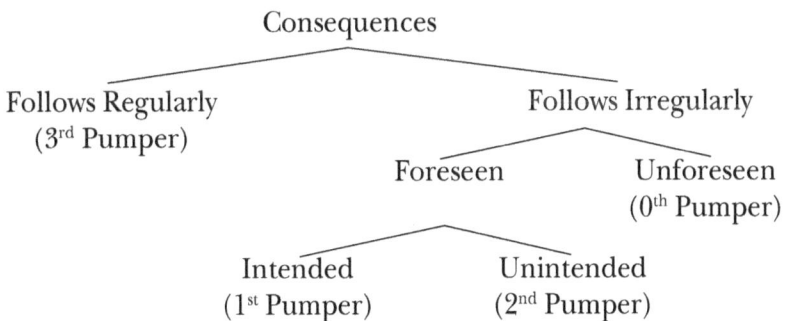

Consequences

Follows Regularly
(3rd Pumper)

Follows Irregularly

Foreseen

Unforeseen
(0th Pumper)

Intended
(1st Pumper)

Unintended
(2nd Pumper)

We might wonder why we should defend the second pumper at all: if we are going to hold him responsible for the ill effect of his action, why should we absolve him of doing it intentionally?[29] Here, I take it, is Anscombe's way through. She wants to insist that in some, perhaps in many, cases the ill effects of our actions should be avoided even if, properly speaking, they fall outside of our intention. Following Aquinas, we are held morally responsible for all foreseen and all ordinary unforeseen effects. But a defense we can make for those effects for which we must answer (by Aquinas' lights) but which we do not count as intended (by Anscombe's lights), is that the only alternative would have been to *intentionally* commit evil. There is no illicit proportionalism or consequentialism here, however: we can absolve someone whose (in)action results in the death of thousands if the only alternative available to him were, e.g., to kill a single innocent. The kind of proportional reasoning which is here acceptable is asking, "What must I do to avoid this unordinary ill effect?"

And here the old moral slogan applies: it is better to suffer than to commit injustice, one cannot intentionally commit an evil action even in order to avoid the unintended ill effects of one's avoidance. So that even the aim for which we act is neither sufficient nor determining: those actions from which evil effects ordinarily result must be avoided according to their kind. In this way Anscombe's rulings in her examples can be saved but also rendered more defensible, so that we can capture more fully how her account accords with Pius' words with which we began.

---

[29] Anscombe considers precisely this protest (§ 25, p. 45).

References

Anscombe, G. E. M. (1963). *Intention* (2nd ed.). Cambridge, MA: Harvard University Press.

Anscombe, G. E. M. (1982). Medalist's Address: Action, Intention and 'Double Effect'. *Proceedings of the American Catholic Philosophical Association, 56,* 12-25.

Aquinas, T. (1920). *Summa Theologiae* (Fathers-of-the-English-Dominican-Province, Trans.).

Aquinas, T. (1995). *On Evil* (J. A. Oesterle & J. T. Oesterle, Trans.). Notre Dame, IN: University of Notre Dame Press.

Aquinas, T. (1999). *Commentary on Aristotle's Physics* (R. J. Blackwell, R. J. Spath & W. E. Thirlkel, Trans.). Notre Dame, IN: Dumb Ox Books.

Aristotle. (1995). *Complete Works* (J. Barnes Ed.). Princeton, NJ, USA: Princeton University Press.

Balme, D. M. (1987). Aristotle's biology was not essentialist. In A. Gotthelf & J. G. Lennox (Eds.), *Philosophical Issues in Aristotle's Biology* (pp. 291-312). Cambridge: Cambridge University Press.

Finnis, J. (2011a). Anscombe on Spirit and Intention *Intention and Identity: Collected Essays* (Vol. 2, pp. 69-78). Oxford: Oxford University Press.

Finnis, J. (2011b). Intention and Side Effects *Intention and Identity: Collected Essays* (Vol. 2, pp. 173-197). Oxford: Oxford University Press.

Foot, P. (1967). The Problem of Abortion and the Doctrine of the Double Effect. *Oxford Review*(5).

Frey, C. (2007). Organic Unity and the Matter of Man. *Oxford Studies in Ancient Philosophy*, 167-204.

Kelsey, S. (2010). Hylomorphism in Aristotle's Physics. *Ancient Philosophy, 30,* 107-124.

Lennox, J. G. (2001). Material and Formal Natures in Aristotle's *De Partibus Animalium Aristotle's Philosophy of Biology* (pp. 182-204). Cambridge: Cambridge University Press.

McDowell, J. (1996). *Mind and World*. Cambridge MA: Harvard University Press.

O'Brien, M. B., & Koons, R. C. (2012). Objects of Intention: A Hylomorphic Critique of the New Natural Law Theory. *American Catholic Philosophical Quarterly, 86*(4), 655- 703.

Pius-XII. (1952). On the Moral Limits of Medical Research and Treatment. Retrieved 09/13/14, from http://www.papalencyclicals.net/Pius12/P12PSYCH.HTM

Thompson, M. (2008). *Life and Action*. Cambridge, MA: Harvard University Press.

Vogler, C. (2013). Good and Bad in Human Action. *Proceedings of the American Catholic Philosophical Association, 87*, 57-68.

6. The Ethical Relevance of the Intended/Foreseen Distinction According to Anscombe

T.A. Cavanaugh

In her magisterial "Modern Moral Philosophy" (henceforth, *MMP*), G.E.M. Anscombe writes that:

> The denial of any distinction between foreseen and intended consequences, as far as responsibility is concerned, was not made by Sidgwick in developing any one 'method of ethics;' he made this important move on behalf of everybody and just on its own account; and I think it plausible to suggest that this move on the part of Sidgwick explains the difference between old-fashioned utilitarianism and that consequentialism, as I name it, which marks him and every English academic philosopher since him. By it, the kind of consideration which formerly would have been regarded as a temptation, the kind of considerations urged upon men by wives and flattering friends, was given a status by moral philosophers in their theories. (Anscombe, 1958, p. 12)

In *MMP* and elsewhere, Anscombe proposes the intended/ foreseen (or I/F) distinction as crucial to resisting the descent into consequentialism (an ethical theory whose name she coins in the above passage). Speaking most precisely, the I/F distinction contrasts the intentional from what is voluntary but not intentional:

> Something is voluntary though not intentional if it is the antecedently known concomitant of one's intentional action, so that one could have prevented it if one would have given up the action; but it is not intentional: one rejects the question 'Why?' in its connexion. (Anscombe, 2000, section 49, p. 89)

In disputes concerning the I/F distinction, one encounters three contested issues. First, how does one go about distinguishing intent from foresight? Second, how does one apply this distinction so as to vindicate the classic parsing of cases such that, for example, terror bombing of civilians counts as intended (and is, thereby, prohibited) while consequentially comparable tactical bombing that concomitantly kills non-combatants counts as foreseen but not intended (and is not, thereby, prohibited)?[1] Third, and perhaps most importantly,

---

[1] In her (presumably first published) treatment of double effect as an undergraduate in 1939 at twenty or so years of age (one notes she included it in her collected papers and acknowledges in her introduction to the same that she wrote this part of a pamphlet co-authored with Norman Daniels), we find:

> It has been argued that it is justifiable to attack civilians because their death is an example of "double effect". But this is no example of double effect, which is exemplified when an action designed to produce one effect produces another as well by accident. If, for example, a military target is being attacked and in the course of the attack civilians are also destroyed, then their destruction is not wicked, for it is accidental. Obviously, before their destruction can be passed over on these grounds, it must also be shown that the action is of sufficient importance to allow such grave incidental effects. No action can be excused whose consequences involve a greater evil than the good of the action itself, whether these consequences are accidental or not [here the text has a footnote citing Aquinas' founding account of double effect, *Summa theologiae* IIaIIae, q.64, a.7; Anscombe translates the relevant passage as: "The force used must be proportioned

what moral relevance, if any, does this distinction have? That is, even if terror bombing does differ from consequentially comparable tactical bombing as the intended differs from the foreseen, why think that this difference makes for a moral difference between the two types of bombing such that terror bombing is nowise permissible while tactical bombing, further considerations such as necessity being met, is permissible?

In this paper, I address this third question by presenting what I take to be Anscombe's account of the ethical relevance of the I/F distinction. I note at the outset that the bulk of Anscombe's discussion of the I/F distinction does not concern this question. Indeed, to call her suggestions an account (might) go a little too far – particularly when one considers her work as it bears on the first two questions. For, concerning those issues Anscombe has extensive answers, found particularly in *Intention*, her insuperable treatment of action.[2] However,

---

to the necessity."] Double effect therefore only excuses a grave incidental consequence where the balance of the total effects of an action is on the side of the good. (1981a, p. 78)
One notes that by "accidental" Anscombe has "not essential to the morality of the act" not "by accident" in mind; otherwise, the "must also be shown" would be otiose.

[2]In *Intention*, Anscombe understands herself to be addressing questions that have ethical import, but that precede ethics. So, for example, we find: "As for the importance of considering the motives of an action, as opposed to considering the intention, I am very glad not to be writing either ethics or literary criticism, to which this question belongs" (Anscombe, 2000, section 12, p. 19). Elsewhere, she writes, "Now if intention is all important – as it is – in determining the goodness or badness of an action..." (Anscombe, 1981b, p. 59). Clearly, as she herself indicates in *MMP*, the fruit of work in moral psychology will largely be found in its bearing on ethics properly. That is, in the moral evaluation of acts and agents. One must look closely in her work to discern precisely why she regards intent as having the moral import she clearly ascribes to it. In *Intention*, for example, one tends to find only intimations of ethical import, such as: "Of course we have a special interest in human actions; but *what* is it that we have a special interest in here?" (original emphasis, 2000, section 46, p.83). Ethics constitutes the special interest; moral psychology defines the noted *what* or subject matter, namely, action.

as she insists, the distinction is critical. Thus, what she does have to say about its moral import, albeit less extensive and somewhat piecemeal, merits our consideration.

In Anscombe's work, the most pressing reason for recourse to the I/F distinction depends upon the absolute prohibition of certain acts, no matter the consequences of not so acting ("do justice, even if the heavens fall" or *fiat justitia, ruat coelum*). In Anscombe's account, these exceptionless prohibitions give us reasons for granting the I/F distinction ethical significance. Thus, I will first look at the relationship she sees as obtaining between absolute prohibitions and the distinction.

The I/F Distinction and the Absolutely Prohibited: Refusals and Doings

We find Anscombe locating the moral import of the I/F distinction (partially) in its support of absolute prohibitions:

> The distinction between the intended, and the merely foreseen, effects of a voluntary action is indeed absolutely essential to Christian ethics. For Christianity forbids a number of things as being bad in themselves. But if I am answerable for the foreseen consequences of an action or refusal, as much as for the action itself, then these prohibitions will break down. If someone innocent will die unless I do a wicked thing, then on this view I am his murderer in refusing: so that all that is left to me is to weigh up evils. Here the theologian steps in with the principle of double effect and says: "No, you are no murderer, if the man's death was neither your aim nor your chosen means, and if you had to act in the way that led to it or else do something absolutely forbidden." Without understanding of this principle, anything can be – and is wont to be – justified, and the Christian teaching that in no circumstances may one commit murder, adultery,

apostasy (to give a few examples) goes by the board. ...the prohibitions are bedrock, and without them the Christian ethic goes to pieces. Hence the necessity of the notion of double effect (Anscombe, 1981b, p. 58).

Anscombe proposes to employ the I/F distinction to prevent absolute prohibitions from breaking down, under their own weight, as it were.[3] She considers two paths by which they might break down *via* foreseen consequences associated with either what one refuses to do or with what one does. Since she herself first considers the case of foreseen consequences associated with what one refuses to do, let us do so, too. We will then consider the second case of foreseen consequences associated with what one does. (One notes that historically[4]

---

[3]In *Intention*, Anscombe notes that only negative, prohibitive practical (in the sense of governing what we seek and avoid) principles can be universal. She notes that the premise, "Do everything conducive to not having a car crash," is, "an insane," premise:

> For there are usually a hundred different and incompatible things conducive to not having a car crash; such as, perhaps, driving into the private gateway immediately on your left and abandoning your car there, and driving into the private gateway immediately on your right and abandoning the car there.

She goes on to note that, "Only negative general premises can hope to avoid insanity of this sort" (2000, section 33, pp. 58-61).

[4]The *locus classicus* of double effect is St. Thomas Aquinas' discussion of a private individual's act of self-defense that results in the death of his assailant. One finds this in *Summa theologiae*, IIaIIae, q.64, a.7 (Aquinas, 1962). One must note that Aquinas has a very complex account of licit killing in general and licit self-defense in particular that grants great import to distinctions (and their interaction amongst one another) between: legitimately authorized (public) killing/not legitimately authorized killing, self-defense/defense-of-others, private individual/public official, and *intentionem/praeter intentionem*. Absent public authorities granting private individuals the authority to kill in self-defense (as, for example, our authorities appear to have done throughout the U.S.), the natural law does not grant private individuals the authority to kill intentionally, even in self-defense. Public officials, however, may intend to kill in self-defense *qua* public officials. With respect to self and other-defense, Aquinas inherits an account that understands St. Augustine to hold (correctly) that one may kill in defense of others but not in defense of self. For the former

and to this day typically, while the I/F distinction does apply to what we allow, one finds it principally employed in cases of what one causes.)[5]

Refusals

Let's flesh out the example a little by borrowing a famous case from Bernard Williams:

> Jim finds himself in the central square of a small South American town. Tied up against the wall are a row of twenty Indians, most terrified, a few defiant, in front of them several armed men in uniform. A heavy man in a sweat stained khaki shirt turns out to be the captain in charge and, after a good deal of questioning of Jim which establishes that he got there by accident while on a botanical expedition, explains that the Indians are a random group of the inhabitants who, after recent acts of protest against the government, are just about to be killed to remind other possible protestors of the advantages of not protesting. However, since Jim is an honoured visitor from another land, the captain is happy to offer him a guest's privilege of killing one of the Indians himself. If Jim accepts, then as a special mark of the occasion, the other

---

instantiates proper love of neighbor while the latter instances inordinate love of self over neighbor. St. Thomas proposes that, properly understood, St. Augustine (and the true account) holds that one may defend oneself with the, "moderation of a blameless defense," as long as one does not intend to kill the assailant. If the assailant dies, the defensive act is licit. For one has a greater responsibility to preserve one's own life than that of another. Needless to say, Aquinas' account requires (and merits and repays) much study. For a consideration of Thomas' account, see, e.g., T. A. Cavanaugh (2006, pp. 1-37).

[5]The standard use of the distinction in association with double effect concerns cases such as tactical bombing that concomitantly kills civilians, hysterectomy of a cancerous gravid uterus that concomitantly kills the baby, and palliative terminal sedation that concomitantly kills the patient whose pain is relieved. For a consideration of double effect and allowing, see Cavanaugh (2006, pp. 166-177).

Indians will be let off. Of course, if Jim refuses, then there is no special occasion, and Pedro here will do what he was about to do when Jim arrived, and kill them all. Jim, with some desperate recollection of schoolboy fiction, wonders whether if he got hold of a gun, he could hold the captain, Pedro and the rest of the soldiers to threat, but it is quite clear from the set-up that nothing of the sort is going to work: any attempt at that sort of thing will mean that all the Indians will be killed, and himself. The men against the wall, and the other villagers understand the situation, and are obviously begging him to accept. What should he do? (Williams, 1982, pp. 98-99)

Anscombe holds that Jim should obey the absolute prohibition not intentionally to kill the innocent. He should not accept the, "guest's privilege," of killing one of the Indians. Rather, he should refuse to kill the one Indian. Thereby, he will obey the absolute prohibition of not murdering. If he does refuse, however, he might appear to bear responsibility for Pedro's murdering of all twenty. Does he, in effect, murder nineteen by not murdering one? If this were the case, it would seem that all that is left for him is the weighing up of the evil of his one murder *versus* Pedro's twenty. Thus, it would seem that Jim ought to murder one in order to spare nineteen.

The accusation that Jim murders nineteen, however, fails. For while he foresees their deaths as inevitably resulting from his refusal, he does not intend the deaths of the nineteen either as an end or as a means. Anscombe's response illustrates both the exculpatory and the justificatory character of the I/F distinction. Consider what Anscombe would say to Jim: "No, you are no murderer, if the man's death was neither your aim nor your chosen means, and if you had to act in the way that led to it or else do something absolutely forbidden" (Anscombe, 1981b, p. 58).

In his refusal, Jim does not murder. For, as Anscombe (2005b, p. 262) notes:

> We cannot offer a sharp and simple definition of murder. But there is a central part of its extension which can be reasonably well-defined, namely, the intentional killing of the innocent. Whenever this is done by rulers, soldiers, terrorists or other violent men, reference is made, in reporting it, to the murder of innocent victims. This gives us one of our paradigms of the murderer, and constitutes the hard core of the concept of murder.[6]

Moreover, as Anscombe remarks, if saving the nineteen requires his deliberately killing the one innocent, then in addition to being excused from the accusation of murder, he is justified in his refusal. For the only alternative is to murder. Thus, the distinction between what one has responsibility for as intended as an end or means and what one has responsibility for as foreseen but not intended proves crucial in sustaining exceptionless prohibitions.

Now, in order to distinguish this kind of case from other salient cases having to do with the need for the I/F distinction, I will call it the *challenge of retortion*. More customarily, one might hear it referred to as the *moral blackmail* case. I prefer 'retortion' as it shows the almost logical need for the I/F distinction. As Anscombe puts it, without the distinction, the "prohibitions will break down." I would add, under their own weight. Of course, the I/F distinction addresses the problem of

---

[6]Also, "murder is the deliberate killing of the innocent, whether for its own sake or as a means to some further end" (Anscombe, 1981b, p. 53). Thus, the hard core is the intentional killing of the innocent (not simply intentional killing). Anscombe notes (and I concur) that public officers may legitimately intend to kill: The idea that they [rulers and their subordinates] may lawfully do what they do, but should not *intend* the death of those they attack, has been put forward and, when suitably expressed, may seem high-minded. But someone who can fool himself into this twist of thought will fool himself into justifying anything, however atrocious, by means of it (1981b, p. 54, note 2).

moral blackmail; I do not deny its relevance. A response to the challenge of retortion addresses something much more basic, however. That is a logical question; namely, when employed on themselves (and, I would add, on one another, to address cases in which one pits, e.g., adultery over against murder), do the absolute prohibitions continue to make sense? For example, the claim that "nothing is true" breaks down when applied to itself. Thus, the I/F distinction plays a crucial role in addressing the very first challenge that absolute prohibitions face, their logical tenability when turned on themselves.

The second scenario that Anscombe suggests concerns not what we refuse to do, but what we do. As noted, historically and in the contemporary debate, this is actually the topography from which double effect first arose. That is, Aquinas first muted the issue of double effect and, in his terms the intended/ besides intention (*intentionem/praeter intentionem*) distinction as it bears on one's doing or causing that produces two effects, one intended and one besides one's intention. Let us consider such cases.

Causings

The issue of deaths that one actually causes leads Anscombe to introduce what she calls her, "principle of side effects."[7] The role the I/F distinction plays in refusals differs from that it

---

[7]She does so because certain salient abuses of double effect (attributable on the one hand to Cartesianism and, on the other, to Proportionalism) make her shy of endorsing double effect. For the most salient forms of it she encounters are corrupt. Indeed, Anscombe says, "Now, to make an epigram, the corruption of non-Catholic moral thought has consisted in the denial of this doctrine, and the corruption of Catholic thought in the abuse of it" (Anscombe, 2005a, p. 247). Also, we read: "we are touching on the principle of "double effect". The denial of this has been the corruption of non-Catholic thought, and its abuse the corruption of Catholic thought" (Anscombe, 1981b, p. 54). For an extensive discussion of the relation between her "Principle of Side Effects" and double effect, see Cavanaugh, (forthcoming).

plays in doings. For in retortion we face a logical, conceptual challenge, as it were. In causings we face what we may call material or practical implications. That is, do common causings violate the exceptionless prohibition?

With this question in mind, let us turn to Anscombe. On the occasion of her receipt of the Aquinas Medal, Anscombe proposes her, "principle of side-effects:"

> I will call it the 'principle of side-effects' that the prohibition on murder does not cover *all* bringing about of deaths which are not intended. Not that such deaths aren't often murder. But the quite clear and certain prohibition on intentional killing (with the relevant 'public' exceptions) does not catch you when your action brings about an unintended death. (original emphasis, Anscombe, 1982, p. 21)

Given the sensibility of an absolute prohibition against murder, the principle of side-effects (or something like it) becomes necessary. For, otherwise, as Anscombe (1982, p. 20) illustrates the point, "you can't build roads and fast vehicles, you can't have various sports and races, you can't have ships voyaging over the seas, without its being predictable that there will be deaths resulting." So, the principle of side effects defines the set of cases that are not necessarily wrong (as intentional killings of the innocent). As she notes, "the principle is modest: it says 'where you must not aim at someone's death, causing it does not *necessarily* incur guilt'" (original emphasis, Anscombe, 1982, p. 20). She elaborates, saying:

> The principle is unexceptionably illustrated by some examples of dangerous surgery, by some closings of doors to contain fire or water; or by having ships and airlines. In these we are helped by thinking of the deaths as either remote or uncertain. (1982, p. 21)

Anscombe notes that the principle of side effects, "does not say *when* you may foreseeably cause death" (original emphasis, 1982, p. 22). However, the above-mentioned unexceptionable cases with reference to the remoteness or uncertainty of the outcomes suggest that we have two features to focus upon: the remoteness of the foreseen bad outcome or its uncertainty.

Take remoteness first.[8] Consider flood doors in a submarine. When closed to prevent the deaths of the entire crew (and the submarine's sinking), the deaths of the submariners in the flooded section (although certain) are remote. For one closes the doors and at some remove (causally and temporally, subsequent to the compartment's filling with water), the submariners die. The submariners die with certainty, but at some remove from the closing of the doors.

Now, take uncertainty. To consider examples Anscombe herself proposes, we legitimately fly airplanes, launch ships, build roads and manufacture cars although we know that doing so will result in the deaths of innocents. For while those deaths are foreseen with statistical certitude they are not individually foreseen as certain. For example, we know with (statistical) certitude that given a certain number of flights, a certain number of deaths due to crashes will occur. This certitude does not make flying planes a violation of the absolute prohibition against murder. Were we, however, to fly a specific plane knowing with certainty that its flying would result in the deaths of innocents, we would be culpable of murder, regardless of our not intending that result.

From the above, it appears as if the principle of side effects complemented by the remoteness (not a, "near consequence,") or lack of certainty of the foreseen outcome secures permissibility of the contemplated action. This appears to me to be the import of Professor Anscombe's principle of side effects whereby the I/F distinction has ethical import insofar as it delimits unobjectionable

---

[8]This and the following paragraph rely on Cavanaugh, forthcoming.

foreseeable causings of the deaths of the innocent.[9] We can drive cars, close flood and fire doors, fly planes, launch ships, build bridges, perform surgery, and so on. For while we foresee deaths concomitant upon such acts as either remote or uncertain, we do not intend them either as a means or end. Thereby, we do not violate the prohibition against murder in such (otherwise unobjectionable) doings.

Thus, along with Anscombe, we see that absolute prohibitions rely on the I/F distinction to address questions associated with both acts of refusal and causation. Thereby, we discern grounds for granting the I/F distinction moral import. Now, in Anscombe's work, a third and allied basis for the ethical relevance of the I/F distinction can be found in the idea of what I will call intrinsic badness. Certainly, the absolute prohibitions concern acts whose badness is found in the acts themselves and not, for example, in a weighing up of their consequences. Nonetheless, we might distinguish the use of the I/F distinction as it bears on absolute prohibitions (both refusals and doings) on the one hand, and the intrinsically bad, on the other, and this for at least two reasons.

First, even if all and only intrinsically bad acts are absolutely forbidden, the denomination differs. That is, we have thus far focused on the absolute nature of the prohibition, not the intrinsic badness of the act. Even if materially or referentially the same, conceptually, or in terms of sense, this is a distinct item. Simply put, it differs in definition. Second, one might think that the category of the intrinsically bad is larger than that of the absolutely forbidden. For example, it may be the case that breaking a promise is intrinsically bad yet does not rise to the level of being absolutely forbidden. Note that this does not mean that it is ethically in the clear to break the relevant promise. It only means that the category of absolutely

---

[9]For a more extensive consideration of her principle of side effects and how it differs from an account of double effect, see Cavanaugh, forthcoming.

prohibited is a limited one meant to capture the most egregious ethical violations. In any case, the category of the intrinsically bad instances a third basis for Anscombe's recourse to the I/F distinction.

Intrinsic Badness

In *MMP*, Anscombe offers an example illustrative of the import of the I/F distinction as it bears on intrinsic badness. I will follow her example in the main, fleshing it out with roles and some narrative context. So, on to the example. A grandfather provides money for the care of his granddaughter whose father ought to provide money, but does not. The grandfather does this due to the death-bed request of his (now-deceased) daughter whose lack of confidence in her husband (the girl's father) as a provider led her to seek such a promise. The granddaughter lives with her decent, albeit Micawberish, father. The grandfather pays her tuition at a private all girl's high school and incidental expenses associated with her extra-curricular activities, including a club swim team also requiring monthly payments. The granddaughter, a freshman, thrives at the (expensive) school and as a swimmer on her club team.

Anscombe stipulates (correctly, I think) that it would be wrong for the grandfather to deliberately, purposefully, intentionally withdraw support for either of two reasons. First, as an end, simply because he no longer wanted to support her. Second, as a means to the good end of compelling her father to support her. Thus, we have the position that the grandfather has a serious obligation to support his granddaughter. This remains so even in the case in which by not supporting her he could force her father to do the right thing. The girl's father, availing himself of the grandfather's promise, neglects to support his daughter financially.

Now, to complicate matters, we have a third act to contemplate that implicates support of the child. Namely, the grandfather's doing something disgraceful and continuing to support the girl or not doing that disgraceful act and going to jail, and thereby foreseeably but not intentionally (either as an end or as a means) withdrawing support. The disgraceful act is not as bad as selfishly withdrawing support. So, let us say that the grandfather is an investigative journalist who faces the prospect of revealing the identity of his source of information at the insistence of a court or contempt of that court and some time in jail during which he cannot support his granddaughter. Let us say (and I realize that this claim might be controverted, but I do not think it outrageous) that revealing this person's identity, while disgraceful as a violation of his professional ethic and of the trust placed in him, would not be as bad as withdrawing support simply because he has tired of the expense and would like to spend money on himself. Note that this judgment of the relative badness of the two acts will particularly hold if we assess the violation of the journalistic ethic not in terms of its intrinsic badness, but in terms of its reasonably expected consequences. (Of course, this is part of Anscombe's point.) Now, with this case in place, what happens if we lack the I/F distinction? Here is Anscombe:

> By Sidgwick's doctrine, there is no difference in his responsibility for ceasing to maintain the child, between the case where he does it for its own sake or as a means to some other purpose, and when it happens as a foreseen but unavoidable consequence of his going to prison rather than do something disgraceful. It follows that he must weigh up the relative badness of withdrawing support from the child and of doing the disgraceful thing; and it may easily be that the disgraceful thing is a less vicious action than intentionally withdrawing support from the child would be; if then the fact that withdrawing support from the child is a side effect of his going to prison does not make any difference to his

responsibility, this consideration will incline him to do the disgraceful thing, which can still be pretty bad. And, of course, once he has started to look at the matter in this light, the only reasonable thing for him to consider will be the consequences and not the intrinsic badness of this or that action. So that, given that he judges reasonably that no *great* harm will come of it, he can do a much more disgraceful thing than deliberately withdrawing support from the child. (original emphasis, 1958, p. 12)

For our purposes, the crucial passage comes where Anscombe notes that, "the only reasonable thing for him to consider will be the consequences and not the intrinsic badness of this or that action." Absent a focus upon intent contrasted from foresight, the intrinsic badness of this or that act plays little to no role in the grandfather's consideration of what to do. For, intent constitutes the intrinsic character of an act – the act itself – in contrast to its reasonably expected consequences. Intent being put to the side, we lose the very idea of the intrinsic badness of this or that action. (Presumably, the same holds concerning an act's intrinsic goodness.) What we will have left over is broadly voluntarily effected reasonably expected consequences. Thus, our agent is left to calculate expected consequences.

When he does set about with his calculations, if our illustration holds, he will arrive at the decision to reveal his source. But Anscombe suggests that this is not where his consequentialist deliberations will end. For, as she says, if the intrinsic badness (at least partially – if not entirely – established by intent) of breaking a father's promise to a dying daughter or violating a profession's ethic does not matter while only reasonably expected consequences do, then will not this grandfather-*cum*-journalist come to judge that he should simply perjure himself before the court? For, thereby, he avoids many reasonably expected bad outcomes (being charged with contempt of court, sentenced to some time in jail, no longer being able to pay his granddaughter's expenses, and all the bad effects upon his granddaughter). Conversely, what are the reasonably expected consequences of perjuring himself in court? Perjury is rarely found out, even more rarely prosecuted, and whom does it harm? Of course, perjury in a court of law on a serious matter (such as the contemplated case – courts not pressing their claims against journalists lightly) would be a "much more disgraceful thing" than deliberately withdrawing support from the child.

Importantly, Anscombe by means of the distinction between intent and foresight introduces a complexity into her example that matches the world (at least as I have come to know it), but for which consequentialism has little patience or sensitivity. Indeed, the intricateness of the example can be a little vexing (even for a sympathetic reader). For she asks us to consider four scenarios, or acts when it comes to our agent. First, one in which he stops supporting his granddaughter simply because he tires of doing so. Second, one in which he stops supporting her in order to compel her father to do the right thing and support her. Third, one in which his abiding by his profession's ethic and not revealing his journalistic source earns him contempt of court and jail time in which he can no longer offer support. Fourth, his act of perjuring himself under oath in court. I take it that part of the point of the numerous acts is to contrast their intrinsic badness, which can only be got at by means of intent.

Consider the different ways in which these four acts are intrinsically bad in contrast to bad in terms of their reasonably expected results. The first act breaks the promise of a father to his dying daughter in her role as mother and originates from a callous selfish motive ("I'm done writing these endless checks"). In terms of its (reasonably expected) consequences, it distresses an adolescent and has a certain probability of getting a father to do the right thing by his daughter. The second act breaks the same promise while embodying an admirable intent ("He needs to grow up and support his daughter; I am simply enabling him to neglect his financial responsibilities towards her"). It also distresses an adolescent and has a similar probability of getting a father to do the right thing. The third act of honoring a professional ethic is intrinsically admirable; it involves as a foreseen but not intended consequence distressing an adolescent. The fourth act involves perjury (more explicitly defined as speaking a falsehood with the intent of deceiving) in a serious matter before a court of law while having numerous concrete good consequences (avoiding jail time, not revealing a journalistic source, not distressing a young girl) and speculative bad ones (the harm that comes from countenancing perjury in court).

Absent the I/F distinction and in light of the reasonably expected consequences outlined above, we do descend, as Anscombe proposes, into consequentialism. Of course, the consequentialist will not regard this as an argument on behalf of the moral import of the distinction. Anscombe, however, does. Moreover, she rightly does so insofar as we clearly can and readily do assess, respectively, the above four acts in themselves, as selfish, understandable but misguided, admirable but costly, and shamefully unjust. Indeed, the I/F distinction captures these very aspects of our judgments concerning the above four acts. Consider them in order.

First, for our agent to break his promise to his deceased daughter simply because he tires of it is selfish, callous, pusillanimous, and greedy. The intent of having more for one's self at the cost of a needy other defines (and thereby condemns) it. Second, for him to break his promise in order to get his former son-in-law to do the right thing – while verging on the honorable – is understandable, but misguided. Certainly, the improvident father should support his daughter. Moreover, his former father-in-law should try to get him to do so. However, he ought not to use the breaking of his promise as a (bad) means to that good end. Third, for a journalist to refuse to reveal his source to the court is admirable, heroic, civilized, the kind of liberty on account of which men willingly risk their lives and for which songs are written and sung. It is regrettable that he and his granddaughter shall suffer for it, but mature decisions come at the expense of those who make them. We admire those who make such decisions for what they intentionally do while foreseeing the associated costs. Fourth, and finally, to perjure oneself is to say what one knows is false with the intent of deceiving. Inherently unjust, it further miscarries and obstructs justice. For this reason, the decent consider it disgraceful.

The distinction between what we intend as an end or as a means and what we foresee as associated with what we intend structures the above act-evaluations. Yet, if we do not contrast intent from foresight, we must cast aside the very idea of the intrinsic badness of an act. This leaves us bereft of all but consequentialism's banal approach. In contrast to that gross weighing up of consequences, Anscombe proposes a refined moral vocabulary referencing virtue and vice. Virtue and vice and their relationship to intent serve as a further basis for the moral import of the I/F distinction, as we will now see.

Intent, Virtue, and Vice

At the end of *MMP* (1958, pp. 8-9), Anscombe proposes that:

> It would be a great improvement if, instead of "morally wrong," one always names a genus such as "untruthful," "unchaste," "unjust." We should no longer ask whether doing something was "wrong," passing directly from some description of an action to this notion; we should ask whether, e.g., it was unjust; and the answer would sometimes be clear at once.

In this memorable passage, Anscombe exhorts us to recover richer act-descriptions than the overly general right or wrong, moral/immoral, permissible/impermissible categories. (Not to speak of the even more superficial consequentialist, "overall more productive of good than of bad/overall more productive of bad than of good.") Rather, she admonishes us to use categories such as virtuous/vicious – the actual categories we find ourselves and others employing when we speak of acts and agents as honest or deceitful, thoughtful or obtuse, considerate or manipulative, generous or selfish, and so on. Earlier in *MMP* she had noted that consequentialism is inevitably a "shallow" philosophy. It is so, in part, because it evaluates acts in these very general terms, as right or wrong, or, as all things considered beneficent or maleficent. Yet, absent a focus on intent, one has only the voluntary (in Aristotle's sense of what one knows and wills) to determine what is subject to moral evaluation. Now, as Aristotle says, decision best instances virtue (and vice). Indeed, as the very definition of virtue indicates, deliberate decision exemplifies the essence of virtue (and vice).[10] What is deliberate decision? Well, another word for it is intent. The intended is what we have deliberately decided upon. It concerns our ends and our means to our ends. Hence, intent instances virtue and vice.

For example, to consider a few vicious acts, to utter a falsehood with the intention of misleading is deceitful. To treat another solely as a means of venereal pleasure is lustful. To speak in order to embarrass is spiteful. To harm another for one's own delight is sadistic. To consider a few virtues, to give with the intent of relieving suffering is tender-hearted or merciful (*misericordiae*). To overcome fear in order to preserve a threatened good is courageous. To tell a joke in order to delight is humorous. And so on. Intent captures the virtue or vice of our acts. For the deliberately decided

---

[10]Aristotle, *Nicomachean Ethics*, "virtue is a habit of deciding" (1106b36).

upon, the intended, exemplifies virtue and vice. We may find here, too, that the opponent parts ways with us and with Anscombe. So be it. Absent the ethical import of intent (and, thereby, when relevant, how it differs ethically from foresight), act-evaluations must remain shallow, general, and, ultimately, not very informative. In not acknowledging the moral import of intent, the consequentialist can speak of acts only as, all things considered, beneficent or, all things considered, maleficent. That is, the consequentialist can only say, net, the act produced good or, net, the act produced bad. Needless to say, this is a highly impoverished moral vocabulary.

In the above four reasons for acknowledging the moral import of the I/F distinction (to recount them they are: 1) absolute prohibitions: refusals; 2) doings; 3) intrinsic badness; and, 4) virtue and vice), the consequentialist will probably not find one convincing argument. This does not impute the quality of Miss Anscombe's arguments. Indeed, she would probably take it to recommend them, distinctly. Nonetheless, one would like to have some argument to offer based on ground shared with the consequentialist. This brings me to the fifth and final Anscombian reason for granting the I/F distinction's moral relevance. I myself believe it is the most important reason, but perhaps the least developed in her account, although it remains implicit in large portions of her impressive *oeuvre*.

The Presumptive Moral Import of Moral Psychology

The final basis for the ethical import of the I/F distinction is not explicitly stated by Anscombe. Rather, it is the overall significance of her insistence in *MMP* that we get a sound moral psychology before we do ethics.[11] Moral psychology

---

[11]A reader familiar with the ponds of ink devoted to the topic of switching trolleys cannot but be struck in reading *Intention* to find: "Switching (on, off)" as exemplifying a description *not* dependent on the, "form of description

(action theory) investigates the ontology of actions and the distinctions of which they admit. In *Intention* Anscombe speaks of our, "special interest in human actions" (Anscombe, 2000, section 46, p. 83). That special interest is called ethics. Ethics evaluates the very actions that moral psychology defines and differentiates. Simply put, distinctions of which actions admit (action-theory distinctions) presumptively make for differences within act-evaluation (ethics) because, as action-relevant distinctions, generally and thereby, they mark morally important differences. Just as distinctions amongst living things make for biologically important differences (such as the difference between those living things that produce sexually and those that produce asexually), and distinctions amongst health systems (such as that between respiration and circulation) make for important differences amongst physicians (such as that between pulmonologists and cardiologists), so, too, differences amongst acts such as that between the intended and the voluntary *prima facie* make for ethically important differences such as that between consequentially comparable terror and tactical bombing.

In effect, the consequentialist grants moral import principally to one and only one action-theory distinction. That is the distinction between the voluntary and the not voluntary. Indeed, ethics is about the voluntary; roughly, what we may refer to along Aristotelian lines as knowing-willing. Indubitably, morality assesses what we knowingly and willingly cause or allow. This is true, as far as it goes. The problem is that it

---

'intentional actions'" (Anscombe, 2000, section 47, p. 85). The point is not that switching is not an action, nor even that it is not at times an intentional action. Anscombe, of course, holds that such a description could apply to an intentional action. The point is, rather, that a paradigmatic action in contemporary ethics is one that liminally counts as an act. The ethics that preoccupies itself with discussing such impoverished threshold instances of action is unlikely to escape a similar poverty in its own act-assessments.

does not go far enough. For, as Anscombe repeatedly shows us, within the voluntary there are important differences. In particular, there is the difference between what we might refer to as the intended, on the one hand, and the simply voluntary, on the other. Of course, the intended is simply voluntary, so the difference is not one of what is present in the voluntary being absent in the intended. Rather, in the intended we find ourselves knowing willing our knowing willing. That is, we deliberate concerning what we want; upon the completion of deliberation we intend our end and the means to it. Intending is one of those acts that we take concerning our own action. It exemplifies the properly human act of rising above our own acts and taking them as our object. It resembles the way in which we not only know, but we know that we know; we not only want, but we have wants concerning our wants (e.g. that they be good). It is in intention that we find the properly ethical. By that I mean we are no longer contrasting what is subject to moral appraisal from what is not (as we do with the distinction that establishes morality, that between the voluntary and the not voluntary.) Rather, we here find distinctions within the voluntary. In this sense, they are properly ethical distinctions, occurring entirely within morality.

The mind boggles to think that these distinctions would lack ethical relevance, considering that they are simply articulations or ramifications of one side of the first morally relevant distinction. Namely, that between what is voluntary and is, accordingly, subject to moral appraisal and that which is not and is, accordingly, not subject to ethical evaluation. While not explicitly stated by Miss Anscombe, this is the point and purpose of her insuperable (and countless) contributions to moral psychology and, in turn, to any sound morality. In other words, moral psychology is morally important psychology. That this (dare we call it analytic?) point has entirely been lost indicates our desperate need for her profound insights. Deeply in her debt we remain.

References

Anscombe, G. E. M. (1958). Modern moral philosophy. *Philosophy*, 33, 1-19.

Anscombe, G. E. M. (1981a). The justice of the present war examined. In Anscombe, G. E. M. (1981) *The collected philosophical papers of G. E. M. Anscombe* (Vol. 3) (pp. 72-81). Oxford, UK: Basil Blackwell.

Anscombe, G. E. M. (1981b). War and murder. In Anscombe, G. E. M. (1981) *The collected philosophical papers of G. E. M. Anscombe* (Vol. 3) (pp. 51-61). Oxford, UK: Basil Blackwell.

Anscombe, G. E. M. (1982). Medalist's address: Action, intention and 'double effect'. *Proceedings of the American Catholic philosophical association*, 56, 12-25.

Anscombe, G. E. M. (2000). *Intention* (2nd ed.). Cambridge, MA: Harvard University Press.

Anscombe, G. E. M. (2005a). Glanville Williams' *the sanctity of life and the criminal law*: A review. In Geach, M., & Gormally, L. (Eds.), *Human life, action and ethics: Essays by G. E. M. Anscombe* (pp. 243-248). Exeter, UK: Imprint Academic; St. Andrews Studies in Philosophy and Public Affairs.

Anscombe, G. E. M. (2005b). Murder and the morality of euthanasia. In Geach, M., & Gormally, L. (Eds.), *Human life, action and ethics: Essays by G. E. M. Anscombe* (pp. 261-277). Exeter, UK: Imprint Academic; St. Andrews Studies in Philosophy and Public Affairs.

Aquinas, Thomas (1962). *Summa theologiae*. Roma, IT: *Editiones Paulinae*.

Aristotle (1990). *Nicomachean Ethics*. (H. Rackham, Trans.). Cambridge, MA: Harvard University Press.

Cavanaugh, T. A. (2006). *Double-effect reasoning: Doing good and avoiding evil*. Oxford, UK: Clarendon Press.

Cavanaugh, T. A. (forthcoming). Abuses of double effect, Anscombe's principle of side effects, and a (sound) account of *duplex effectus*. In O'Callaghan, J., & Iffland, C.

(Eds.), *Intention and double effect: Theoretical and practical challenges*. Notre Dame, IN: University of Notre Dame Press.

Williams, B. (1982). A critique of utilitarianism. In Smart, J. J. C., & Williams, B. (1982). *Utilitarianism for and against* (pp. 75-150). Cambridge, UK: Cambridge University Press.

Part 4

Anscombe on Embryos,
Souls, and Persons

7. Anscombe on Embryos and Persons

David Hershenov & Rose Hershenov

A nscombe's "The Early Embryo: Theoretical Doubts and Practical Certainties,"[1] as well as other essays, appeals, to some extent, to an Aristotelian/Thomistic argument of *mediate animation* (aka *delayed hominization*). On the unadulterated Thomistic view, the pregnant woman's womb is the location for a succession of souls, ending eventually with the rational soul of a human being. This conforms to her belief that while the embryo is an individual thing, an organized body, it is not a human being due to a lack of features and organs (2008, p. 214). She also considers monozygotic twinning to pose significant problems to the claim that the early human embryo is a very young human being. Consequently, she argues, though very tentatively, that the earliest human embryo is not a human being. And yet, it nonetheless shares the same

---

[1]Printed in *Faith in a Hard Ground: Essays on Religion, Philosophy and Ethics* by G.E.M Anscombe ed. by Mary Geach and Luke Gormally, Imprint Academic Center, 2008, pp. 214-223.

life as a future human being. To injure or kill the embryo in its mother's womb eight and a half months before it was born would have been to harm it. She writes "You would be wronging the prospective human being even by something done to *him* at a stage – if there is such a stage – so early that he was not yet one" (2008, p. 223) and "you can wrong someone by what you do to, say, an early cell cluster which was a stage in *his* development" (2008, p. 223). Her position is based on what she claims to be an (admittedly strange) neo-Aristotelian argument in which there is a time that the early embryo is not of any species of animal; therefore her modified succession of souls does not involve substantial change (2008, p. 217). She concludes, then, that to end the *life* of an embryo is to end the *life* of the human being.

We will argue here that while it may be a common misinterpretation of Anscombe to claim that she maintains that you were never an early embryo or zygote, she did believe that you did exist then, just not as a human being. Her argument, then, allows for a prohibition on ending the lives of embryos while refraining from the (bold) claim that embryos are human beings. And this, Anscombe claims, is the extent of the Church's mandate on the treatment of embryos: embryos are not (yet) specifically argued to be human beings, but we must nonetheless treat them as such. Hers, then, is a theory on embryos that offers philosophical support for precisely what the Church teaches.

In this paper we will present Anscombe's argument and demonstrate her philosophical support of the Church's mandate that we treat embryos as one of us. We explore her notion that there is a life that is not yet the life of a human being but will later be the life of a human being. Since Anscombe elicits support from Aquinas, whom she deems to be "intrinsically worth referring to in this context," we will present then a Thomistic argument for rational ensoulment at fertilization. This, we will argue, is compatible with the basic tenets of Anscombe's theory, but is distinct from it in that it places the origin of the human being at fertilization. To do so, we will argue that Aquinas' neo-Aristotelian embryology was—as Anscombe notes—erroneous, and that his delay of rational ensoulment is based on this. We will claim that Thomistic metaphysics applied to modern embryology renders much more plausible the embryo having a rational soul from fertilization onwards even in cases of monozygotic twinning.

On Anscombe's account, there was, at one point, *something* human—a zygote—and yet this human substance that was a zygote was not *a* human. Nor was it more than one human.[2] The zygote was *you* however, and we believe that Anscombe thought of 'human being' as a phase sortal, rather than a substance sortal. She sees 'human being' as referring to something that you are identical to, but not essentially, in the same way that you can be identical to a teenager but you are not essentially one. The phase "human being" begins after twinning is no longer possible, and the embryo bears the marks of a human body, both of which happen early in development.

What persists from the zygote stage to the beginning of the human being phase of your existence is the "life." In "Were you a Zygote?" Anscombe claims that, in the case of the zygote, this existence or life is not that of the sperm and egg, which fused to form the zygote, but that of the zygote itself, a "new kind of thing from what they were" (1984, p. 115). She writes, "the two lives of the sperm and the ovum have ended because they have turned into an individual with a new life, the life carried by the zygote" (1984, p. 115). Here, then, marks the substantial change, wherein the new human substance begins to exist. On her view, the life is carried by a soul, yet, as she writes in "The

---

[2] "Were You a Zygote?" Royal Institute of Philosophy Lecture Series / Volume 18 / September 1984, pp 111-115.

Early Embryo", there is a "certain lack of determinateness. This one zygote will very likely develop, if all goes well, into one single human being, but it may also develop into more" (2008, p. 221). This soul, then, is a soul that has a life and, when united to the proximate matter that is the fertilized egg, brings into existence a human substance. But she does not yet want to say that it is a human being, and so she draws upon the Aristotelian-Thomistic tradition of delayed hominization. Her delayed hominization, however, does not involve the substantial change that comes with the Thomistic succession of souls. And in order to reject substantial change, she draws on a move that both Aristotle and Aquinas (using Aristotle's metaphysics) make, wherein in the process of production, there is animal soul that does not belong to any specific kind of animal, "there is a stage of living with animal life without being, for example, a man or a horse" (2008, p. 217). She thinks that if Aquinas can suppose this—that you can have an undetermined animal soul, an animal without any particular species, become an animal of a certain species—then one need not consider the embryonic developmental changes from vegetative to animal to rational life to involve substantial changes. Anscombe writes:

> Why can't I say that I am the same *living thing* as that zygote? If in its development it could come alive with animal life without having the substantial form of any particular kind of animal, then why should we respect the argument that change from vegetative life to animal life is substantial change, and therefore involves the cessation of what is change and the start – the coming to be – of the new thing it changed into? After discovering what Aquinas was prepared to say about a certain stage of animal life, he seemed to me to be unjustified in inferring a substantial change in the way that I have indicated. (2008, pp. 217-18)

What she seems to believe, then, is that there is a soul present that manifests first vegetative life, then animal life, and ultimately rational capacities. The soul is united to matter to form a human substance that is a human zygote and then an embryo, but not a human being. It is with the formation of organs, the end of the possibility of twinning, and the beginning of human features, that something first becomes a human being. This is one version of delayed hominization, wherein there is a human substance that is not a human being until late in embryonic development (she imagines around 6 weeks; the whole of embryonic development is 8 weeks long). In other words, she does not believe that a new soul enters with the beginning of the phase "human being." No substantial change has taken place, but the embryo now has been configured so that it is a rational animal, or human being.

While Anscombe uses Aquinas' undetermined animal soul as a justification for her removal of substantial change, her explanation for how this might happen is more detailed and relies on final and formal causes. At its earliest stage, the embryo manifests a unity that she attributes to the soul. And yet this unity is undetermined, for after fertilization, what appears to be a single embryo may "twin" and divide into two or more embryos, or monozygotic twins. Because of this lack of determinacy, where what appears to be a single zygote can divide into twins, she believes that:

> To say that there is here an individualized actual form so operative that we can say of the zygote, 'Here is a human' seems to be too bold. The form that is to be, if development is normal, that is surely what is governing the development at least until you are really justified in saying, 'This is a human.' Now a form that is to be is, as governing a development, is precisely a final cause. (2008, p. 221)

All of the actions done during the first few weeks of the human embryo's life are done for the sake of the "new and coming animal life."[3] It is not, she writes, "like the principle of unity in the life of nutrition and growth, the formal cause" (2005, p. 57). Rather, an animal would be indicated by sensation and movement. So, this new and coming animal life will be that of a rational animal, a human being, marked by the "production of the beating heart, of the inchoate sense organs, of the limbs and of the brains; the existence of almost all of which is necessary if there is to be the life of the animal" (2005, p. 57). This would be at approximately 6 weeks or so after fertilization.

One may ask though, as she does in a title of her essay, "Were You a Zygote?" In other words, were you the product of the fusion of the sperm and egg, a unicellular organism? Her answer is that yes, you were a zygote, and a human one. But you were not yet a human being. For Anscombe, a new life originates with the new human substance that comes into existence at fertilization. The zygote that is this new human substance persists as the *same* substance but does not become a *human being* until after twinning is no longer possible. Again, we read her as viewing *human being* as a phase sortal: just as the teenager does not begin to exist when the human substance reaches adolescence, the human being existed earlier before the human substance became a human being and the rational soul begins to inform matter.

Because you were once a zygote, although not yet a human being, when she brings up a practical matter of litigation, wherein a damaged adult sued a hospital for damage done at an embryonic stage, she writes, "of course you would be wronging the prospective human being even by something

---

[3] "Embryos and Final Causes" in *Human Life, Action and Ethics: Essays by G.E.M Anscombe*. Eds. Mary Geach and Luke Gormally, Imprint Academic, 2005, pp. 45-58.

done to him at a stage—if there is such a stage—so early that he was not yet one" (2008 p. 223). She does not see the human zygote as a human being, but it is the same substance as the later human being and so would be the same subject of harm.

Anscombe's view is, she notes, in keeping with the Church's teaching on the treatment of human embryos, which is that while it has never taught that procuring an abortion during the first few weeks of development is permissible, the Church has also never committed herself to the thesis that the rational soul of a human being is there from the moment of conception (or fertilization). We believe with some certainty that she used the Church's position as a guide in her inquiries, for she writes that, with regard to the litigation mentioned above, she was "pleased to note that...the Magisterium of the Church has not 'committed itself to an affirmation of a philosophical nature'" (2008, p. 223). However, she also finds her metaphysical explanation of early embryonic development to avoid complications that come with both twinning and what she considers to be physical signs that the early embryo is not yet a human being: its lack of organs and its outward form.

There are many things to appreciate about Anscombe's position. For Catholics, here is a substantial philosophical position that supports the Church's prohibition on early abortions without providing the embryo the status of 'human being.' This is no small feat, for the problems that come with monozygotic twinning are a puzzle for philosophers defending the zygote as a human being. On Anscombe's account, though, the zygote is merely a human substance, not yet a human being, and so can divide without violating the persistence conditions of human beings. In other words, the problem with the early embryo being one of us is that it can divide into two, as happens with monozygotic twinning, when the embryo divides into two identical embryos. Since we cannot divide into two and survive, it seems that the embryo cannot be one of us. However, Anscombe's point is that it is not "one" of us. It is not a human being, but a human substance, which can divide, for "we cannot say that we have here two distinct animals. But we can say that we have two materially distinct carriers of the life that started with the formation of the zygote" (1984, p. 115). This is a main point of hers: the early embryo is not a *single* human substance that is identical to a single human being. Rather, it is a human substance that can give rise to two or more human beings, eventually, all which share in the life of that original human substance. So, as she writes, "for identical twins, they were jointly something human, and then each severally something human" (1984. p. 114).

One of our interests here is to propose a solution to twinning that has the human being existing as the human zygote. Our solution will actually be, at face value, much like Jerome Lejuene's solution, which Anscombe explicitly rejects. However, the similarities are superficial, for our solution rests upon what we believe to be a robust metaphysical analysis of early embryology, one which allows for us to have once existed as zygotes, and to survive the twinning phase as the same human being that will eventually become the fetus, neonate, etc. We will offer a Thomistic metaphysics, but will separate Aquinas' analysis of embryology from the erroneous Aristotelian science that he used to construct his original theory of delayed hominization.

First, though, we will look briefly at possible solutions to twinning, all of which Anscombe rejects, except for the last. They are as follows:

(1) Lejuene's solution: both twins are present from fertilization onwards, and split at some point. Anscombe finds no sufficient evidence for this, and wonders, if this were true, what sort of metaphysical status this entity might have that is not one, but two human beings, for by Lejeune's account, the twinning

imprint would be on all zygotes. She thinks there is no proof for it and thinks there may not even be proof against.

(2) The Sprouting Solution: the original zygote was not yet divided, but "grew" a sibling, one that is days younger despite being an identical twin. Anscombe rejects this largely because there is no evidence, and, as with Lejeune's solution, if this budding were imprinted on the zygote, its metaphysical status as something destined to twin renders it, at the least, a curious phenomenon.

(3) Fissioning (and fissioning out of existence): There is a single human being that fissions into two identical human beings. This, Anscombe charges, carries with it a host of problems, including the possibility of each set of twins, the products of fission, costing a sibling (the original zygote), to fission out of existence.

(4) Pre-embryo solution: There is a zygote and embryo that is not a human being but an early embryo that can twin into human beings. This is what some philosophers would term a "pre-embryo." This "pre-embryo" solution is the one Anscombe most favors, for she argues that the early embryo is not a human being, but is a human substance.

Our own solution is a Thomistic one, and, to present it, we will turn briefly to his own metaphysical account of embryology. Aquinas's metaphysical analysis of embryology was erroneous, as Anscombe notes, for he uses Aristotle's science, which has no conception—no pun intended—of the fusion of the sperm and the egg, and the resulting zygote. Rather, Aquinas tries to explain what might happen when the female menstrual blood is formed by the male semen into what is at first a substance with vegetative life, then one with animal, or sensitive life, and then finally a human being. This is his theory of delayed hominization, or "succession of souls", in which there is first a sensitive soul, then an animal soul, and finally the human being's rational soul, which is the point of hominization, when the human substance comes into existence.

We think, though, that with a proper Thomistic analysis of embryology, we can position hominization at fertilization. Aquinas' soul is a rational soul, and it is this soul, or form, when united with matter, that is the human being. It is a "subsistent" substance, for it can exist without matter after death, albeit in a deprived state (this is not a capacity it has, though, prior to the creation of the human being. When created it is necessarily united to matter). And, on Aquinas' hierarchy of being, the human being stands on the border of the corporeal and incorporeal worlds, a metaphysical amphibian, positioned between the "dumb" animals and the angels. This privileged position is ascribed to it because of the human soul's powers of intellect and will, which Aquinas argues are not reducible to matter and so renders it transcendent. In fact, Aquinas argues that although the human form begins to exist in its natural state of configuring matter, it will exist when separated from matter at death, albeit in a deprived state (ST I q.76; q. 90 a. 4).[4]

What is relevant to our argument is that the rational soul is not a "thinking" soul, but an ontic structure whose powers, or potentialities, are rationality, sensitivity, and vegetation. The essence of the soul is not reducible to these potentialities, and Aquinas goes to some trouble to make this distinction. The advent of new activities of an ensouled substance does not indicate that a new substance has come into existence; rather it is the manifestation of powers that are had by the soul: "… if the very essence of the soul were its immediate source of operation, whatever has a soul would also have actual vital

[4]St. Thomas Aquinas, 1948: *Summa Theologiae I*. Trans. English Dominican Fathers. New York: Benzinger Brothers.

actions, as that which has a soul is always an actually living thing" (ST I q. 77 a.5).

The soul is the "first act," the fundamental ontic structure in which the operations are rooted. The "second act" is the actual operations of the powers, and it is the substance itself that is more appropriately called their subject (SCG II q. 59).[5] This is because souls require matter for their full operation. In his discussion of angels, Aquinas makes this point about the rational powers explicit, and extends it to other creatures, "Neither in an angel nor in any creature, is the power or operative faculty the same as its essence...the angel's essence is not his power of intelligence: nor is the essence of any creature its power of operation" (ST I q. 54 a.20). The powers are potentialities that the soul has, that are not always active, but are capable of being manifested if united to matter in the proper way.

Aquinas' distinction between the essence of the soul and its powers affords Aquinas' metaphysics a human soul that can exist *without* thinking, and so allows for a human embryo that has a rational soul. The sense of "rational" that is used to describe the human soul refers to a kind of ontic structure, then, which gives rise to rational activity through its configuration of matter. In fact, the configuration of matter—the development of a body, or substance—is to produce a body that will allow for the manifestation of the soul's specific powers. And, reflecting the hierarchy of being, the first powers manifested are the vegetative, followed by the sensitive (or animal powers), and then rational powers. But this succession of powers does not necessitate a succession of souls, or mediate animation, nor does it render ad hoc the claim that it is the rational soul present throughout all

[5]St. Thomas Aquinas, 1923: *The Summa contra Gentiles of St. Thomas Aquinas, Book II* trans. English Dominican Fathers. London: Burns, Oates and Washburn.

of embryonic development, and the fetal, neonate, etc. It is the soul that configures the matter, and the substance that is the soul, and matter develops as it does—into a being that manifests rationality—*because* of the rational soul's acting upon the matter.

It makes little sense, then, to claim that the rational soul is bestowed at some point in embryonic development after fertilization simply because rational faculties are not yet manifested. Anscombe does not make this specific point, but she does posit the rational soul as a final cause rather than an organizing principle. Again, she writes about the early stage where a human substance is present but not yet a human being:

> What is governing here is the principle of unity of a new and coming life, the animal life of movement and sensation which is not yet there. But one cannot doubt that what is done—the action of the living embryo in its earliest stages—is done for the development of that animal life—the production of the beating heart, of the inchoate sense organs, of the limbs, of the brain; the existence of almost all of which is necessary if there is to be the life of an animal....Heart, brains and sense organs there must be. (2005, p. 57)

And even if the animal life precedes the presence of the rational life, this still happens very early on: "...I incline to rely on its outward form and its having the human organs. In fact, I suppose that the period of animal but not yet human life must be very short. I have seen it reported that a six-week-old conceptus has been observed to swim vigorously with a breast stroke..." (2008, p. 217). Surprisingly, on Anscombe's account, the advent of the human being phase, or hominization, precedes the manifestations of a rational life by several months.

The looming problem, of course, is the problem of monozygotic twinning, or the apparent division of a single embryo into two embryos. Here we will offer a solution to monozygotic twinning. Like Lejuene's solution, we believe that there are two souls present, and as the embryos grow, they divide and split into two separate embryos. Sometimes, of course this splitting is not successful, and the twins are conjoined (which will actually help our case). However, in most instances, twins separate and continue as two genetically identical individuals.

Our account, though, is made more robust than Lejeune's with a Thomistic metaphysics. The rational soul, on Aquinas' account, is on the boundary of the corporeal and incorporeal world, and, like the angels, can exist without matter. This happens in the afterlife. Of course, it is not a separate substance, but a subsistent one, but it nonetheless shares some of its characteristics with the angelic forms. One of these is how it is individualized, or what its principle of individuation is. To see this, we can see how, for all creatures, the act of existence is conferred from without, for the only being whose essence is His existence is God. All other beings are given their existence from God, and so even the angelic and human forms stand in potentiality in terms of existence. Aquinas writes, "Each being possesses its act of existing and its individuation in accordance with the same factor" (QDA I a.2).[6] It is the form that receives its existence and imparts that existence that it receives from the composite— or in the case of the separate forms, simply retains it. That the form is the individuating principle, because it receives existence, allows then for the individuation of angels, of departed souls, and for the only Being whose existence is His essence: God.

There is, however, the famous "designated matter" reference of Aquinas,' which is often understood as the principle of individuation, at least for corporeal beings. Joseph Owens,

---

[6]St. Thomas Aquinas, 1984: *Quaestiones De Anima*. Transl. James H. Robb. Milwaukee: Marquette University Press.

who advocates the formal individuation thesis, argues that the dimensions of the matter do individuate at some level, but these dimensions are due to a prior cause: the form, first, and even more fundamentally, the existence that the form confers to the substance, and hence the matter.[7] And Aquinas makes the following comment in his Treatise on Man:

> The soul communicates that being, in which it subsists to the corporeal matter, out of which, with the intellectual soul, there results one being; so that the being of the whole composite is also the being of the soul itself. This is not the case for other forms, which are not subsistent. For this reason, the human soul retains its own being after the dissolution of the body, whereas other forms do not. (ST I q. 76 a.2)

What *this* affords us, then, is a soul that has its own principle of individuation apart from matter. And so, with twins, we say that there are two, as we say, spatially co-located souls, or even overlapping souls, that appear as one body, the zygote or early embryo. Both twins are present at fertilization; in cases of twinning, the "designated matter" is deceptive. For human beings, the individuation lies with the soul, and so there are two souls united to matter, and hence, on a hylomorphic account, two human beings. So, in cases of twinning, two human beings come into existence at fertilization when two souls are infused into the unicellular body. Upon infusion, the souls of each of these bodies are collocated, sharing the same matter. Each of these twins, a composite of matter and form, is a human being, and as the matter is configured by each form, the two human beings usually separate. However, in some cases, the twins do not separate and are conjoined. Every theory of ensoulment will have to accept, in the cases

---

[7]Joseph Owens, 1988: 'Thomas Aquinas: Dimensive Quality as Individuating Principle', *Mediaeval Studies*, 50, pp. 279-310.

of conjoined twins, considerable overlap of two souls sharing the same matter. Many cases of conjoined twins have massive overlap. Our theory just begins with total overlap. And so on this account, monozygotic multiples were both (or all) present at fertilization, and in typical cases, separate during the first two weeks or so after fertilization. And in all cases, the human being, the composite of matter and form, is present at fertilization.

There are, we believe, several merits to this view. One is that there is actually evidence (as Anscombe seeks in her inquiries about Lejeune) for the claim that there is either collocation or overlap of two human beings prior to twinning. This was one of her criticisms of Lejeuene's view, that there was no evidence that both twins are present from the beginning. In some cases of conjoined twins, there is major overlap or even collocation of organisms. The extreme dicephalus, which shares a body but has two heads, had one vegetative life for quite a while after Anscombe's threshold for the beginning of the human being. What eventually individuates is the rational power, since the dicephalus may always share a body, and so a vegetative life, but they do not share a mind. Since there do not seem to be two life processes, even when they are fully developed, we believe that these were two collocated souls at one point that eventually merely overlap, although to a large extent.

Another merit to a collocation view, as part of a theory of immediate hominization, is that it preserves our status as essentially "rational animals." On Anscombe's delayed hominization view, we exist *before* hominization, or before we become a human being, and so are contingently rather than essentially rational animals. We exist, then, before we are a rational animal, which runs contrary to Aristotle and Aquinas, but, perhaps more importantly, to Church teaching.

Finally, a collocation theory of twinning is also neater than other solutions. On this view, we can still have the zygote and embryos as human beings, and no one dies, or fissions out of existence, when twinning occurs. Twins do not come at the cost of a genetically identical sibling. And if twinning is determined from the beginning, then Anscombe's view entails that there are necessarily human substances who are never going to become human beings. Their status would be morally like gametes, for it would be impossible for them to ever become human beings. So if twinning is determined, this would be one of Anscombe's problems. Ending the life of a human substance that is destined to twin—if this is how twinning works—would be merely akin to contraception, for the human substance that would be destined to twin would have no more chance of becoming a human being than would a gamete.

Anscombe worried that pro-lifers put too much stake into the metaphysical status of the human embryo, for if they are wrong about this, and it is not a human being, then they can offer no protection for it. She writes, "Suppose the thesis *were* proved wrong? Would all these stalwarts say, "Oh well then, say, up to four weeks then, you can kill it?" (2008, p. 218). Hers is a theory that prevents painting oneself into a corner, and supports the Church's teaching, for she shows how you need not have a human being present during these strange early days when twinning is possible and when an animal life is not obviously present. We hope to have advanced her endeavors by presenting a view that preserves the protection of the zygote and embryo as one of us.

References

Anscombe, G.E.M. (1984). "Were You a Zygote?". *Royal Institute of Philosophy Lecture Series,*18, pp 111-115.

Anscombe, G.E.M., (2005). "Embryos and Final Causes". In Mary Geach and Luke Gormally (Eds.), *Human Life, Action and Ethics: Essays by G.E.M Anscombe* (pp. 45-58). United Kingdom: Imprint Academy.

Anscombe, G.E.M. (2008). "The Early Embryo: Theoretical Doubts and Practical Certainties". In Mary Geach and Luke Gormally (Eds.), *Faith in a Hard Ground: Essays on Religion, Philosophy and Ethics* (pp. 214-223). United Kingdom: Imprint Academic Center.

Aquinas, Thomas (1923). *The Summa contra Gentiles of St. Thomas Aquinas, BookII* (English Dominican Fathers Trans.). London: Burns, Oates and Washburn.

Aquinas, Thomas. (1948). *Summa Theologiae Book I*. (English Dominican Fathers, Trans.). New York, NY: Benzinger Brothers.

Aquinas, Thomas (1984). *Quaestiones De Anima*. (James H. Robb, Trans.). Milwaulkee: Marquette University Press.

Owens, Joseph 1988. Thomas Aquinas: Dimensive Quantity as Individuating Principle. *Mediaeval Studies, 50*, pp. 279-310.

8. How Much Ontological Baggage Do Religious Practices Carry? Anscombe on Prayer to and for the Pre-resurrected Dead

Michael Staron & Peter Furlong

Ontologists continue formulating rival accounts of the human person, basing their theories off of their experience of the world and the things in it. As Catholics, however, there are additional factors at play. In this paper, we are going to be focusing on one, namely, the practices of praying to and for the dead prior to the resurrection. For this reason, we will examine a number of views that Catholics may reject due to other considerations. In section 1, we will outline a number of rival accounts of the human person and consider them in light of the practices of praying to and for the dead. As we will see, each account either runs into difficulty with regard to these practices or faces general philosophical problems. In section 2, we will turn to the views of Elizabeth Anscombe as presented in her 1950's paper "The Immortality of the Soul." As we will see, Anscombe's views differ from the contemporary rival accounts about disembodied persons in some interesting ways. In section 3, we will discuss some advantages and disadvantages of Anscombe's views.

1. Ontological Accounts of the Human Person

The first category we will consider includes two different theories: materialism and what we will call thin hylomorphism. By "materialism" we mean the theory that human persons are purely material beings. The materialist may admit that there are beings that are immaterial either in whole or in part, but maintains that humans are not among them. The second theory requires a bit more explanation. First, consider hylomorphism. According to the hylomorphist, the human person, like all corporeal substances, is composed of form and matter. We wish to distinguish between two different versions of this theory: thin hylomorphism and thick hylomorphism. According to the thin variety, the substantial forms of substances cannot exist without accompanying matter; according to the thick variety, human souls, the substantial forms of humans, can exist without matter. Aquinas provides a clear example of a thick hylomorphist, while Aristotle may have endorsed a kind of thin hylomorphism, although his position on the matter is difficult to ascertain (see Miller, 2012).

We consider thin hylomorphism together with materialism because adherents of both positions agree that substances cease to exist at death and possess no immaterial parts that may survive on their own. Both of these views face a problem with the practices of praying to and for the dead: There are no dead to pray either to or for. There may, however, be ways around this problem, and we will consider one such possibility.

Perhaps one could respond that through the grace of God, the living are able to interact with people after they have been resurrected. There may be no more problem in trying to communicate to those who are currently experiencing a temporal gap in their existence than in writing a letter to one's future descendants, although there may be reasons for thinking that such temporal gaps are impossible. The problem arises concerning how the dead respond to such prayers. One should be wary of invoking backwards causation, even with the help of divine assistance; instead, the adherent of this position would do well to lean on divine foreknowledge. Perhaps God just knows that the resurrected-dead will pray for the living, and so he takes this into account before it happens.

It is unclear whether this or any other solution ultimately resolves the difficulties that materialists and thin hylomorphists face concerning the practices of praying to and for the dead. In the end, we do not mean to argue that the materialist and thin hylomorphist cannot possibly account for these practices, but only that they face some difficulties that must be addressed. Additionally, Christian materialists and thin hylomorphists face difficulties with the possibility of the resurrection: It seems as if any attempt at resurrection, no matter how God brings this about, will result in the production of doppelgangers or duplicates rather than in the revivification of the dead (Van Inwagen, 1978). A number of solutions have been offered to this difficulty. The most infamous of these requires God to "snatch" bodies, or some part thereof, preserving them from decomposition until the resurrection (Van Inwagen, 1978). Others have suggested other solutions requiring less bizarre divine action, but it is unclear whether any of these can satisfactorily solve the problem (Zimmerman, 1999; Hershenov, 2003).

The second category we wish to consider includes two kinds of thick hylomorphism. According to thick hylomorphism, the substantial form of the human being is able to survive separation from the body. We need to distinguish between two different versions of this account. Both versions agree that the soul survives death; they disagree, however, about whether the human person survives. Consider first the corruptionist view, according to which a human person is always constituted by both form and matter. The soul, that is the substantial form, survives death, but the person does not. According to a number of scholars, this is Aquinas's view (Kenny, 1993; Pasnau, 2002; Toner, 2009, 2010).

There is an oddity about this view that arises in light of these prayer practices. Julia may think, for example, that she prays to Saint John, but she actually does not. Saint John no longer exists (although he will after the resurrection). What she prays to is not a person at all. Instead, she prays to Saint John's soul. This is surely odd, and we suspect this is not how most ordinary Catholics think of their practices. Despite this, perhaps the picture is not too bad. The soul, on this view, possesses the intellect and will, which are the most important features of the person. Thus, Julia prays to something that is intimately related to St. John and indeed possesses his most important powers. Still, this view will likely be too much for some to stomach, unless, that is, there is no better option.

On the second version of thick hylomorphism, both the soul and the person survive death. On this account, the substantial form of a human being is sufficient for the existence of a human person. The human soul exists after death, and so too, then, must the human person. This view has also been attributed to Aquinas (Stump, 2003; Brown, 2005, 2007; Oderberg, 2012) and has recently found several contemporary defenders, most notably David Oderberg (2008, 2012). On one leading version of this account, the human person is normally constituted by matter and a substantial form. After death, the person is still constituted, but now by only a single thing, the soul (Stump, 2003). According to this account, like that discussed earlier, a person is not identical to a soul. A soul is, however, sufficient for a person's existence. For this account to work, one must maintain that constitution is not identity. When the person is constituted by two elements, soul and body, it is nonetheless not identical to these two elements. Similarly, when the body is destroyed, the person is constituted by a single element, the soul, but is nonetheless not identical to it.

This view can make sense of the practices of praying to and for the dead, but it seems to face independent problems. It is not clear that the claims about constitution in general are true. It is hard to blame philosophers for wondering just how a thing, constituted by a single entity, is not identical to that entity. Moreover, this view seems to require rejecting the Weak Supplementation Principle, which states that if an object has a proper part x, it must also contain a second proper part that is both distinct from and does not overlap x. Being forced to reject a widely held principle of mereology certainly seems to be a cost, although in the end this may not be as bad as it appears (see Oderberg, 2012). This view then, although it can deal with the practices of praying to and for the dead, faces other difficulties that may make some metaphysicians wary of adopting it.

The third category of theories we wish to examine is that of substance dualism. According to the views we will look at, both the soul and the body are substances. There are, of course, many varieties of substance dualism. We will set aside most of these differences and focus on a single question: How is a human being composed? Here we will distinguish three different answers, and so three varieties of substance dualism: (1) the person is sometimes composed of soul and body, but sometimes is identical to (or constituted solely by) the soul; (2) the person is never composed of the soul and body, but is instead always identical to (or constituted solely by) the soul; and (3) the person is always composed of both soul and body. If one element goes, so too does the person. Olsen refers to the first as "compound dualism" and the second as "pure dualism" and notes that each is often attributed to Descartes, sometimes without any notice of the difference between them (2001). The third view lacks the historical pedigree of the other two, but nothing about dualism itself rules it out. The first and second forms of dualism share an important commitment; according to both, a person exists if and only if his soul exists.

In contrast, the third view is the dualistic analogue of thin hylomorphism; although persons are not purely material, they cease to exist as soon as their bodies do.

If we take the third view, that is, that the human person is always composed of both the soul and the body, then we have a problem we looked at earlier: there are no dead people to pray to or for. On the other two views, we do not have problems for the practices of praying to and for the dead. This may cause a sigh of relief, but this is too quick. Although these practices do not pose new problems, these accounts of the human person have seemed problematic to most metaphysicians. Indeed, the supposed problems with substance dualism are too numerous to discuss in any detail here. Two especially pressing problems concern the nature of the interaction between the soul and the body ("the interaction problem") and the question of which entities are thinking ("the too many thinkers problem"). Here too, then, we are left with a potentially uncomfortable position.

We do not mean to have shown that all of these theories face insurmountable issues. Indeed, we are not convinced that they do. Instead, we wanted to survey some of the major views about the nature of the human person and investigate what problems they face, either in conjunction with the practices of prayer in particular or about their plausibility in general. The purpose of this is to pave the way for consideration of another view entirely, that of G. E. M. Anscombe.

2. An Alternative: Anscombe's View

In "The Immortality of the Soul," Elizabeth Anscombe focuses on the issues under discussion, namely, separated souls, disembodied persons (or what she calls "spirits"), and the practices of praying to and for the dead. First, it is important to note that she affirms both the existence of souls and the existence of separated human souls; as an orthodox Catholic these are existential claims she cannot deny (Anscombe, 2008, p. 77–78). Instead, she begins by considering the following line of reasoning in support of the immortality of the soul. Thinking is an immaterial process. It is an activity that is performed by the immaterial part of us, which is the soul. Since the soul is immaterial, it has it within it to exist without the body. Therefore, we have some philosophical basis for thinking that the soul can survive death. Furthermore, at least when the soul and the body are separated, the soul is an immaterial substance (Anscombe, 2008, pp. 69–71).

Interestingly, Anscombe takes some issue with each of these claims. One of her primary targets in the paper is the claim that we can have some philosophical account of the immortality of the soul. She explicitly denies this. Rather than coming up with theories that account for how the soul can exist disembodied, philosophy should *discourage* people from formulating such accounts. She writes:

> Must one not have a theory of how it [the soul] can exist [after death]? I reply to this that no one can be obliged to have any theories at all; but one may feel irresistibly impelled to have a theory. I have an inclination to say that the good which philosophy can do here would be to cure one of this irresistible impulse. (Anscombe, 2008, p. 78)

Additionally, and importantly for our purposes, she targets the notions of "immaterial part" and "immaterial substance." She says that she has no understanding of the former, and she calls the latter "delusive" (Anscombe, 2008, p. 71). Concerning the notion of an "immaterial part," she says:

> If I am told 'not as the hand is part of a man, because that is a material part, whereas the soul is an *immaterial* part' I can only say that I do not understand; of course it is clear to me that it is not a material part, but then I

do not understand what it means to call it a *part* at all. (Anscombe, 2008, p. 70)

Moreover, relying upon her general understanding of "substance," she argues that the notion of "immaterial substance" is delusive. The category of substance, according to Anscombe, is one where a very specific sort of answer to the question "what is it?" is given— specifically, the name of a substantial kind. Building upon this account, she concludes that the notion of "immaterial substance" is bankrupt:

> It [the notion of substance] relates to the existence of a special restricted sense for the question 'what?' the answer to which is of great practical importance and of great interest to us. The sense is that in which I ask 'what?' when pointing to an unfamiliar tree or plant or rock or parcel of stuff in a jar. The question 'what?' may be asked in such a way that the questioner has no clear conception of the form the answer may take, and it may then receive as answer the name of a substantial kind; or it may expect such an answer and not get it because there is no such answer to give; or it may be definite in quite another way than that of asking for the name of a substance, still there is this special restricted sense, and substances are those things that are named in answer to this restricted sense of 'what?'. The question relates to a certain sort of knowledge that people have, and which is important. It follows that the term 'substance', which serves a very useful purpose here, is out of place where that kind of knowledge is not and cannot be in question. To put it very briefly, a natural object of human knowledge is the *ti esti* (*quod quid est*) of material things: or rather, *ti esti* itself expresses the *form* of one of the most important parts of our natural knowledge. (Anscombe, 2008, pp. 71–72)

So, for example, if we were to point at a plant and ask "what is it?" the answer would be "a plant," and for this reason we can talk about the "substance" of this object and classify this object as a substance. Since the soul is not a material thing, it does not fall within the domain of the natural object of our knowledge—we cannot form conceptions of the *quod quid est* of it, or indeed of any immaterial object. Therefore, the category of substance itself is one which is inappropriate for immaterial realities. Anscombe concludes that the notion of an "immaterial substance" is confused and delusive.

One might be tempted to draw a different conclusion from this line of reasoning. Instead of saying that the category of substance applies only to material realities, why not affirm that the human soul is an immaterial substance and deny that we can know anything *else* about what kind of thing it is? Anscombe considers this position and rejects it. She writes:

> But I do not wish to say: and therefore the *ti esti* (*quod quid est*) of immaterial things is beyond our ken, for although that sounds modest, it in fact unconsciously prejudges the matter. It is as if I were to say: it is only the square roots of *numbers* that *we* are able to calculate; the square roots of metals are not for us; perhaps the angels know them. (Anscombe, 2008, p. 72)

According to Anscombe, our minds are tailored toward knowing material objects, and thus the categorical structures we use are ill-suited for application outside of this range. We must, therefore, refrain from all categorical claims about the immaterial.

It is vital that the relationship between her claims is clear. We cannot appropriately say what the soul is, we cannot appropriately subsume it under a substantial kind, and we cannot do so because it is an immaterial entity. It is for this very reason that we cannot accurately consider them as substances. So while we can say what kind of thing the plant in front of us is—namely, a plant and a substance—we cannot do the same for the soul.

Much of what she says about the soul applies equally well to the disembodied person. She explicitly affirms the existence of such spirits; she believes that disembodied persons exist (Anscombe, 2008, p. 72). However, calling them "immaterial substances" would be just as confused as calling souls "immaterial substances." Her views on this are most manifest when she diagnoses the underlying cause tempting us to categorize spirits as "immaterial substances" in the first place: "The reasons for the special temptation in regard to spirits are, I suggest...that as spirits are persons without bodies, it is natural to apply to them many of the conceptions that we use in connexion with persons, and hence also the *logical* conceptions, and hence that of substance" (Anscombe, 2008, p. 72).

Once again, it is worth highlighting that, according to Anscombe, disembodied persons should not be considered substances for the very same reason that souls should not be considered substances: They are immaterial and, therefore, are beyond our cognitive grasp, so we cannot properly subsume them under a substantial kind. But if we cannot subsume them under our categories, we might begin to wonder what we can say about them. She might say that it depends on the context. Presumably, when talking about specific disembodied persons, at least in certain contexts, she would want us to say that we are talking about particular individuals, for example St. Peter and St. Paul. But what can we say about them ontologically; how would she react to the aforementioned accounts of the human person? Clearly she would reject the different forms of substance-dualism. But what about the hylomorphic accounts we discussed? Is she advocating one of those? It appears not, primarily because she rejects attempts to categorize *what* the disembodied person and soul are; remember, she denies that we can answer the question "what is it?" in contexts where a substantial kind can be given as an answer. The lack of what we can say about them becomes most apparent, interestingly, when she starts discussing petitionary prayer.

Toward the end of her paper, Anscombe brings up petitionary prayer for the first time. It is important to note, first, that she does not discourage the practice in any way; she treats it as well established (see Anscombe, 2008, p. 78). However, in the midst of a dialogue with an imaginary interlocutor, she makes the following claim:

> It may be asked: 'Are you saying that to say the dead exist between death and the resurrection is to say that people pray for and to them?' The answer is, certainly not, but to pray for and to them is to *say* that they exist and I know no other saying that they exist which has any content but that of an *idle* picture or of a superstitious fear or conventional reverence. (Anscombe, 2008, p. 79)

If Anscombe were in favor of any ontological account of the disembodied person, she undoubtedly would have more to say about the dead's existence than that we pray to and for them. But it seems that she does not. Instead, she argues that trying to formulate different ontological accounts of the disembodied person would overstep our bounds and commit us to an "idle picture." In doing so, we would misapply our typical categories that, because of our cognitive limitations, are fit only for classifying material objects.

To summarize, then, Anscombe affirms that the soul exists, that it continues to exist in a disembodied state after death, and that there are disembodied persons. However, all attempts to explain these entities (or even to explain what we are talking about) is based on a confusion. We must avoid subsuming them under our categories—the categories by which we know material objects, such as the category of substance. Philosophy should discourage us from formulating accounts that explain how they can exist and what they are (i.e. what categories they fit into, what substantial kinds they belong to). All the while, we have every reason to maintain our practices of petitionary prayer to and for the dead. These practices can stand by themselves, independent of any ontological account of the disembodied soul. Having outlined her views, we will now consider the costs and benefits associated with them.

3. Costs and Benefits of Anscombe's View

There are advantages to Anscombe's approach. If we shun philosophical accounts of the human soul or the dead in the afterlife, then we avoid all theoretical problems that arise in trying to understand them. Avoiding problems is a virtue for any intellectual move. However, one might get the sense that, by taking her approach, we are throwing the baby out with the bathwater. Instead of avoiding all accounts of the disembodied person and soul because of the theoretical problems that arise, why not keep working until we find one that sidesteps these conceptual difficulties? Or, instead of abandoning all accounts, why not address the earlier difficulties to see if they are as fatal as they appear *prima facie*? Anscombe is not open to such approaches because of her account of the limits of our knowledge. Since we are only apt to know material things, it is inappropriate to even categorize immaterial realities let alone formulate theories about them. Whether Anscombe's understanding of the limits of philosophical explanation is correct is a question far too large to settle in the pages to come. Instead, we will outline a problem that arises internally for Anscombe's theory and relates to the practices of praying to and for the dead.

In "The Immortality of the Soul" Anscombe simultaneously allows for the practices of praying to and for the dead in the afterlife prior to the resurrection and, given her arguments, must deny that anyone should subsume the dead under a substantial kind. However, it is important to recognize that many ordinary Catholics who partake in these practices hold a number of views about the dead. For example, they think they exist, have interests, and hear prayers (presumably through the intervention of God). Additionally, they hold exactly the kind of belief that Anscombe discourages in this paper. Many ordinary Catholics, when asked "what is it?" about disembodied persons in a context where a substantial kind is the appropriate answer, would undoubtedly answer, "human."

A way of making this point is in an imagined scenario. If we pointed to Fido and asked an ordinary Catholic, "what is that?" presumably he would answer "a dog." If we then pointed to a rose outside the window and asked, "what is that?," presumably he would answer "a rose." Likewise, if we then (in this very same context) asked him, "St. Peter in Heaven right now, what is he?" he would say "a human being." He would, that is, subsume St. Peter under the substantial kind "human." This example is a way of drawing out a belief from him, we take it, and it testifies to the fact that many ordinary Catholics do subsume spirits under our typical categories. Undoubtedly Anscombe would allow such an answer in certain contexts, but she would not allow such an answer in an ontological context, i.e. in such a context as described above where we want to know a thing's substantial kind. Given her views on the limits of human knowledge, she needs to discourage the ordinary Catholic from subsuming the dead under one of our typical, everyday substantial kinds; the job of philosophy in this case is to cure the ordinary Catholic from having such thoughts.

Presumably, many ordinary Catholics think that the dead in the afterlife are human because they think that the dead in the afterlife are the *very same humans* as were on earth. This reflects their deeper belief that the individuals to whom and for whom they pray are the *very same individuals or entities* who lived on earth. Interestingly, even though Anscombe does not explicitly discourage this deeper belief in "The Immortality of the Soul," she must reject it based on views she states elsewhere. In her chapter on Aristotle in *Three Philosophers* (1961), immediately after distinguishing first substances (such as herself) from second substances (such as the substantial kind *human*), she writes:

> It will help us to understand this if we remember, and see the mistake in, Locke's doctrine that there is no 'nominal essence' of individuals. Locke said that if you take a proper name, 'A', you can only discover whether A is, say, a man or a cassiowary, by looking to see if A has the properties of a man or a cassiowary. This presupposes that, having grasped the assignment of the proper name 'A', you can know when to use it again, without its being already determined whether 'A' is the proper name of, say, a man, or a cassiowary: as if there were such a thing as *being the same* without *being the same such-and-such*. This is clearly false. (Anscombe & Geach, 1961, p. 8)

There are two things to note about this passage. First, even though it is written in the midst of outlining Aristotle's views, the last sentence shows that Anscombe is expressing her own opinions. Second, it is clearly implied that *being the same such-and-such* means *being the same instance of this substantial kind* since, in this context, she is discussing secondary substances. According to this passage, if we cannot say that an entity is of the same substantial kind from one situation to the next, then we cannot say that it is the same from one situation to the next. Since, as we have seen, she says that we cannot subsume the disembodied dead under a substantial kind, there are no situations in which we can say that they are of the same substantial kind. Consequently, we cannot say that they are the same from one situation to the next and, as a result, that they are the same individuals or entities who lived on earth.

At this juncture, however, it might not seem that there is much of a problem for Anscombe. She discourages people from (a) subsuming the dead under substantial kinds and, as a result,

(b) believing that they are the same individuals or entities that lived on earth, but many ordinary Catholics who pray to and for the dead do both (a) and (b). Why is this problematic? The difficulty becomes evident when we reflect upon how the beliefs of the practitioners relate to the practices themselves: It seems that their beliefs undergird the practices, in the sense that, without the belief that they are praying to and for the very same individuals who lived on earth, the practices of praying to and for the dead lose their intelligibility. For example, the practice of beseeching Saint Peter would not make sense to many practitioners without the belief that the petitioner is beseeching the very same individual who lived on earth. Therefore, by discouraging thinking that the dead in the afterlife are human, she is undercutting beliefs that make the practices intelligible for many ordinary Catholics in the first place.

Before concluding, consider the following Wittgensteinian response to our criticism. According to this response, we misunderstand ordinary beliefs. While ordinary Catholics might utter sentences like "St. Peter in heaven right now is a human being" in certain contexts, these utterances do not express ontologically weighted propositions. Instead, these utterances are just part of the prayer practices themselves. We need to realize, according to this response, that the practices of praying to and for the dead are rather wide ones and include, in certain contexts, utterances like "St. Peter is in heaven right now" and "I believe that St. Peter is in heaven right now." As a result, when an ordinary Catholic answers "human" to the question "what is St. Peter right now?" this answer is not an ontologically weighted one; it is just another move in the "language-game" of prayer (see Wittgentsein, 2001; D.Z. Phillips 2005).

In response, we must ask: If this is not an ontologically weighted context, what is? It is crucial to remember that we are talking about asking a *Catholic* "what is it?" Catholicism is a religion that intentionally makes ontological claims, especially concerning substantial kinds—just think about Christological controversies and subsequent dogmatic pronouncements. So while there might be a case to be made that many ordinary people are not making ontological claims when they assert that someone is human, certainly that is not true for many of the individuals under discussion, who are both Catholic and religious enough to partake in these rather devout practices. Presumably many of these people are informed enough about the faith and have been exposed to enough ontological contexts in their faith formation that this would not be a neutral claim. Of course, (i) we are not saying that this holds true for every devout Catholic practice, (ii) nor do we claim that this holds true for every Catholic who prays to and for the dead, only many of them. Our claims are limited to these specific practices for many Catholics who participate in them. For them, the practices would lose their sensibility given Anscombe's views. As a result, we can say that a certain cost of Anscombe's view is the intelligibility of praying to and for the dead for many of the people who partake in these practices.

Admittedly, this may not be a terrible thing. Maybe she would just encourage them to view matters differently and adjust the practices accordingly. We do not mean to suggest that this criticism is a defeater of Anscombe's views. We only mean to highlight that it is a cost; we cannot keep our practices the way they are, given her views.

References

Anscombe, G. E. M. (2008). The Immortality of the Soul. In M. Geach and L. Gormally (Eds.), *Faith in a Hard Ground* (pp. 69–83). Charlottesville, VA: Imprint Academic.

Anscombe, G. E. M. & Geach, P.T. (1961). *Three Philosophers*. Ithaca, NY: Cornell University Press.

Brown, C. (2005). *Aquinas and the Ship of Theseus: Solving Puzzles about Material Objects*. New York: Continuum.

Brown, C. (2007). Souls, Ships, and Substances: A Response to Toner. *American Catholic Philosophical Quarterly, 81,* 655–668.

Hershenov, D. B. (2003). The Metaphysical Problem of Intermittent Existence and the Possibility of Resurrection. *Faith and Philosophy, 20,* 24–36.

Kenny, A. (1993). *Aquinas on Mind.* London: Routledge.

Miller, F. D. Jr. (2012). Aristotle on the Separability of Mind. In C. Shields (Ed.), *The Oxford Handbook of Aristotle* (pp. 306–339). Oxford: Oxford University Press.

Oderberg, D. S. (2008). *Real Essentialism.* London: Routledge.

Oderberg, D. S. (2012) Survivalism, Curruptionism, and Mereology. *European Journal for Philosophy of Religion, 4,* 1–26.

Olson, E. T. (2001). A Compound of Two Substances. In K. Corcoran (Ed.), *Soul, Body, and Survival: Essays on the Metaphysics of Human Persons* (pp.73–88). Ithaca, NY: Cornell University Press.

Pasnau, R. (2002). *Thomas Aquinas on Human Nature.* Cambridge: Cambridge University Press.

Phillips, D.Z. (2005). Just Say the Word: Magical and Logical Conceptions in Religion. In D.Z. Phillips and M. Von Der Ruhr (Eds.), *Religion and Wittgenstein's Legacy* (p.171–86). Burlington, VA: Ashgate Publishing Company.

Stump, E. (2003). *Aquinas.* London: Routledge.

Toner, P. (2009). Personhood and Death in St. Thomas Aquinas. *History of Philosophy Quarterly, 26,* 121–138.

Toner, P. (2010). St. Thomas Aquinas on Death and the Separated Soul. *Pacific Philosophical Quarterly, 91,* 587–599.

Van Inwagen, P. (1978). The Possibility of Resurrection. *International Journal for the Philosophy of Religion, 9,* 114–121.

Wittgenstein, L. (2001). *Philosophical Investigations.* Malden, MA: Blackwell Publishing Company.

Zimmerman, D. (1999). The Compatibility of Materialism and Survival: The 'Jumping Elevator' Model. *Faith and Philosophy, 16,* 194–212.

9. Anscombe on the Immortality of the Soul

Jeremy Bell

In "The Immortality of the Soul," an early paper that she never published[1], Elizabeth Anscombe vigorously attacks the idea of the "temporal immortality of the soul without the body," declaring it "empty of content" (p.83).

> I take the Christian doctrine of immortality, she says, to be the doctrine of an unending human life, happy or unhappy, after the resurrection, and not the doctrine of an immortal sort of substance, the soul, to which is appended the doctrine of the resurrection because a disembodied soul is not a complete man. (p.77)

At first glance, this may seem flatly inconsistent with Catholic doctrine. Anscombe acknowledges that "our religion teaches us the existence of the souls of the dead between death and the resurrection" (p.78). In describing the idea of the soul's

---

[1] It was published seven years after her death, in Anscombe (2008), pp.69-83. Luke Gormally believes that the paper dates from the late 1950s.

temporal immortality as "empty of content," she does not mean to deny this teaching. She means rather to reject a certain "theory" of *how* souls can exist between death and the resurrection. More fundamentally, she wishes to persuade philosophically-inclined Catholics that no such theory is needed or perhaps even possible.

It is natural to react to these statements with scepticism. Anscombe seems to be making a distinction without a difference. Surely, we may think, "the existence of the souls of the dead between death and the resurrection" straightforwardly *implies* "the temporal immortality of the soul." If Catholicism teaches the first, does it not *ipso facto* teach the second? To speak of the soul's "temporal immortality" is not to advance a theory of how it can exist between death and the resurrection. It is merely to affirm that it *does* exist between death and the resurrection (and, of course, forever thereafter as well). Anscombe would have anticipated this reaction. The move from "the existence of the souls of the dead between death and the resurrection" to "the temporal immortality of the soul" certainly seems innocuous, even compulsory. However, her belief that the latter formula is "empty of content" leads her to deny that the move is innocuous, let alone compulsory. This of course makes it incumbent on her to show that there is a way of accepting "the existence of the souls of the dead between death and the resurrection" while rejecting "temporal immortality of the soul" – and she claims that there is indeed such a way.

My chief interest in this paper is the first claim and I will discuss the second only briefly.

(1) *The idea of the temporal immortality of the soul is empty of content.* The soul, Anscombe observes, is "spoken of as though it were a substance or part of a substance as the hand is part of a man" (p.70). While accepting that the soul is not a part of the human *body*, she professes not to understand what it means to call it a non-bodily "part" of the human being, "at least in a sense

that would justify the thought that it could exist separately."
She does not object to talk of the "immaterial part" (or spiritual
or thinking part) of a human being, remarking that "I...
understand and use such expressions myself."[2] She objects only
to construing these expressions as if they necessarily implied the
soul's "immaterial substantiality," its capacity to exist separately
(p.71). The very conception of an *immaterial substance*," she
says, is "a delusive one."[3] Before examining Anscombe's reasons
for saying this, I must address a preliminary objection. Is she
not illicitly equating the thesis that the soul can exist apart from
the body with the (Cartesian) thesis that it is an immaterial
substance? At least in her later work, she follows Aristotle and
St. Thomas in calling the soul "the form of the body."[4] That the
soul is the form of the body is also Catholic dogma, solemnly
defined at the Council of Vienne (Denzinger, 2002, p.481).[5] If
it is the form of the body, it is not an immaterial substance, even
if it also has the capacity to exist apart from the body. In their
review of *Faith in a Hard Ground*, Michael Pakaluk and Nicholas
Teh accordingly charge Anscombe with "a mistaken conflation
of the Aristotelian-Thomist view with Cartesianism" (Pakaluk
& Teh, 2010, p.488). Though understandable, this objection
seems to me misguided. By "substantiality," Anscombe says she

---

[2]She accepts that thinking is 'not material' (p.69).

[3]At the beginning of the paper she says that she cannot 'at present' accept the
idea that 'spirituality is soulishness itself' (p.69), by which she apparently
means that she cannot 'at present' accept that the soul is an immaterial
substance. (This is what Mary Geach takes her to mean, as she indicates in
her introduction, p.xiv.) Did she later change her mind? To judge by what she
says in the paper 'Analytical Philosophy and the Spirituality of Man', composed
some twenty years later, the answer is no. I discuss this paper briefly below.

[4]See the papers 'Has Mankind One Soul – An Angel Distributed Through
Many Bodies?' (1985), 'Were you a Zygote?' (1984) and 'Embryos and Final
Causes' (1990), in Anscombe (2005), pp.20-21, p.44, p.51 and p.54. See also
'The Early Embryo: Theoretical Doubts and Practical Certainties' (1990), in
Anscombe (2008), p.216.

[5]The wording leaves little doubt that this is a solemn definition, hence that the
doctrine has dogmatic status.

means "a nature in virtue of which it is possible that the soul should exist separate from the body" (Anscombe, 2008, p.70). St. Thomas, no less than Descartes, affirms the "substantiality" of the soul in this broad sense. He denies that the disembodied soul is a "substance" in the sense of something "complete in a specific nature" (Thomas, 1981, p.364), but Anscombe would presumably say that this is not relevant to her difficulties with the notion of the soul's disembodied existence. She is certainly aware of the difference between the Thomist and Cartesian views. She describes the view she wishes to attack as one according to which the soul either is an immaterial substance "or at least exists in the manner of one when it is separate" (Anscombe, 2008, p.71). If the soul "subsists" when separate from the body, as St. Thomas teaches, it "exists in the manner of a substance." (It is therefore not surprising that, on occasion, St. Thomas even calls the soul a "substance," despite its incomplete nature.)[6] This may explain why, as we have seen, Anscombe says that the soul may be conceived as "an immortal sort of *substance*" that is nonetheless "an incomplete man" (and so must be reunited with the body at the resurrection). She is here clearly alluding to the Thomist view, admittedly in slightly misleading language.

Talk of "immaterial substance," for Anscombe, is a misuse or misapplication of the term "substance," whose grammar she discusses at some length. She claims that the term has application in response to "a special restricted sense for the question 'what?', namely, the sense in which a person asks 'what?' when pointing to an unfamiliar tree or plant or rock or parcel of stuff in a jar" (p.71). The question "relates to a certain sort of knowledge that people have;" hence the term "substance" is "out of place where that kind of knowledge is

---

[6]See, e.g., *Summa Theologica* Ia, Q.75, Art.4, Rep. Obj.2; and Q.75, Art.7, 'I answer'. Thomas (1981), p.366, p.369.

not and cannot be in question" (p.72). What is this "certain sort of knowledge?" Anscombe says:

> To put it very briefly, a natural object of human knowledge is the *ti esti* (*quod quid est*) of material things: or rather, *ti esti* itself expresses the *form* of one of the most important parts of our natural knowledge. But I do not wish to say: and therefore the *ti esti* (*quod quid est*) of immaterial things is beyond our ken, for although that sounds modest, it in fact unconsciously prejudges the matter. It is as if I were to say: it is only the square roots of *numbers* that *we* are able to calculate; the square roots of metals are not for us; perhaps the angels know them.

"This," she concludes, "is why I call 'immaterial substance' a delusive conception."

She does not mention St. Thomas in this context, but her statement that "a natural object of human knowledge is the *ti esti* (*quod quid est*) of material things" recalls his dictum that "the proper object of the human intellect...is a quiddity or nature existing in corporeal matter" (Thomas, 1981, p.429).[7] St. Thomas, unlike Anscombe, is prepared to say that the quiddities of immaterial things are "beyond our ken," at least in the present life (*Summa Theologica* Ia, Q.88, Art.2, Rep. Obj.2; Thomas, 1981, p.450). In saying this, of course, he is assuming that we can meaningfully speak of such quiddities, despite not being acquainted with them. Anscombe disagrees. Talk of "the quiddities of immaterial things", in her view, is an instance of what Wittgenstein would call "language going on holiday" (*Philosophical Investigations* I, §38; Wittgenstein, 1958, p.19e). We know what we *mean* when we speak of the

---

[7]Variants on this dictum appear at Q.85, Art.5, Rep. Obj.3; Q.85, Art.8, 'I answer'; Q.87, Art. 2, Rep. Obj.2; and Q.88, Art.3, 'I answer' (Thomas, 1981, p.437, p.439, p.445, p.451).

quiddities of material things, but not when we speak of the quiddities of immaterial things.

Anscombe insists that, in calling immaterial substance a "delusive conception," she is not denying the existence of "spirits" (Anscombe, 2008, p.72). A spirit, she has earlier said, is "a person without a body" (pp.70-71). Evidently she does not consider this a misuse of the term "person." She cautions, however, against the move from "person without a body" to "immaterial person" and from "immaterial person" to "immaterial substance." The "natural" application of the term "substance" is to material things. We lapse into nonsense (not falsehood) if we speak of *immaterial* substance, just as we would if we were to speak of the square roots of metals.

Anscombe does not say that the *sole* natural object of human knowledge is the *ti esti* of material things. It is worth emphasizing that she does not even say we can have no natural knowledge of immaterial things. She says only that we cannot apply to them the category "substance."

The bulk of the discussion of the grammar of "substance" in "The Immortality of the Soul" is reproduced, with minor emendations, in Anscombe's essay on Aristotle in Anscombe & Geach (1961). The context is an exposition of Aristotle's account of substance. Anscombe begins this exposition by stating Aristotle's "very straightforward" doctrine in the *Categories*, according to which its primary sense is "what neither is asserted of nor exists in a subject" (p.7). This definition does not imply that a substance need be material. As Anscombe acknowledges near the end of the chapter, Aristotle himself eventually argues, in Book XII of the *Metaphysics*, for the existence of imperishable and unmoving, hence immaterial, substances (pp.58-59).[8] She says that his argument "seems to contain more than one fallacy,"

---

[8]He is of course by this stage working with a richer conception of "substance" than that found in the *Categories*, but the latter conception has not been jettisoned, only filled in.

but she does not say that its conclusion is *nonsensical*. Nowhere in the chapter does she suggest that "immaterial substance" is a confused misapplication of the term "substance," as Aristotle uses it.

She does, indeed, distinguish the use of the term as a "philosophical technicality" from its use in "ordinary language," though admitting that the two uses are closely related (p.19). The passages adapted from "The Immortality of the Soul" apparently concern only the ordinary use. In delineating the term's grammar in that paper, she seeks to bring the word back to this ordinary use from an objectionable, "metaphysical" use (*Philosophical Investigations* I, §116; Wittgenstein, 1958, p.48e). But she would presumably not say that Aristotle's technical-philosophical use of "substance," his single most important term of art, is nonsensical. She might say the term is meaningful in this use, as in its ordinary use, *only as long as it is not applied to immaterial things*. (The argument in the *Metaphysics* for the existence of "immaterial substances" *would* then be not merely "fallacious" but nonsensical.) But, to show this, she would have to discuss the grammar of this technical-philosophical use of "substance," as well as that of its ordinary use. To repeat, nothing in the "very straightforward" doctrine of the *Categories* suggests that "immaterial substance" would be a misapplication of the term.

On its own, then, Anscombe's appeal to the everyday grammar of the term "substance" does not sustain the charge that the conception of "immaterial substance" is "delusive."

I noted earlier that Anscombe does not deny the possibility of "natural knowledge" of immaterial things. However, she thinks that the expressions "immaterial thing" and "something immaterial" may mislead. She several times compares the soul to numbers. It is "a crude mistake to suppose that the number 2 is a material thing, and this I might conceivably express by saying that the number 2 is immaterial" (Anscombe, 2008, p.70). But she would not call the number 2 an immaterial *substance*. In response to the challenge, "the soul is something, isn't it?" she says, one could not reply "no," for "that would mean that anyone who said anything about souls was talking nonsense, which is evidently false." Nonetheless, "when one has said the 'yes' that is forced by this consideration, one has really said very little." One would equally have to say "yes" to "numbers are something," which is clearly not the same as saying that numbers are substances.

This comparison with numbers is unconvincing. I am doubtful whether most people *would* unhesitatingly say that numbers "are something." Certainly many would deny that they are "entities" or "objects." Anscombe herself implies in her Aristotle chapter that "Are numbers...entities?" is an apparently reasonable question (Anscombe & Geach, 1961, p.20). (It is perhaps not immediately clear what, in general, an "entity" is, but we have some pre-reflective grasp of the concept.) In "On Private Ostensive Definition" (1982b), she attacks the widespread belief that, "if a true proposition has a name as subject and cannot be restated so as not to include such a subject, then we must hold that the subject has an object corresponding to it" (Anscombe, 1982b, p.215). She here uses the term "object" without explanation, apparently in the (vague, pre-reflective) sense of "entity." Frege, for instance, famously held for this reason that numbers are "objects."[9] Anscombe thinks he was mistaken. Whether correct or not, her view is certainly the more intuitive. It is natural to assume that numbers are *not* objects, or entities. By contrast, if one believes in "the existence of the souls of the dead between death and the resurrection," it is natural to assume that "the souls of the dead" *are* entities. Again, if one is prepared to speak of "persons without bodies," it is natural to assume

---

[9]Anscombe here registers a doubt as to whether Frege took numbers to be 'objects' *because* he believed that 'if a true proposition has a name as subject and cannot be restated so as not to include such a subject, then we must hold that the subject has an object corresponding to it'.

that these are entities. Why not say, then, that souls – unlike numbers – are "immaterial substances?"

Anscombe acknowledges the felt difference between souls or spirits, on the one hand, and numbers, on the other. We are tempted to call spirits, but not numbers, "substances," she suggests, because it is natural to apply to "persons without bodies" "many of the conceptions we use in connexion with persons, and hence also the *logical* conceptions, and hence that of substance" (Anscombe, 2008, p.72) . She is apparently suggesting that we apply the "logical conception" (the category) of substance to persons *with* bodies only   *because* they have bodies. *Qua* persons, they are substances only accidentally. But suppose we were to ask Anscombe whether spirits are "entities." As we have seen, she denies that numbers are entities (objects). Would she deny that spirits are entities? Consider certain truths about spirits. The soul of a human being "exists between death and the resurrection." Moreover, it "suffers or is in glory till the resurrection" (p.77). Non-human spirits, as Anscombe says near the end of "The Immortality of the Soul," are either good or evil, and they "play a part in human lives" (pp.82-83). Does it make sense to affirm all of this, but to deny that spirits are "entities?" If Anscombe were to say "yes," the burden of proof would surely be hers. Offhand, it would seem absurd to affirm any of these things about spirits, while yet denying that spirits are "entities." If spirits, unlike numbers, *are* "entities," there seems no reason to deny that they are immaterial "substances," in the "technical" but nonetheless "very straightforward" *Categories* sense.

As we have seen, Anscombe clearly does not consider the expression "person without a body" a sin against grammar. However, she admits that "the idea of a person without a body is fantastic from certain familiar points of view" (p.81). She imagines a comparison with the patently nonsensical idea of a cat or cabbage or table without a body. Is the idea of a person without a body not (thinly) disguised nonsense of the same kind? Anscombe maintains that it is not. However, the claim that "person without a body" *is* a sin against grammar is certainly plausible. It seems *no less plausible* than the claim that "immaterial substance" is such. Undoubtedly, we first learn to apply the terms "person" and "substance" to embodied persons and material substances. The "everyday" use of both terms is confined to visible (material) persons and substances. There is a real difficulty in explaining just how we are able to give any sense to the idea of a person or substance "without a body," if, as St. Thomas teaches, the quiddities of immaterial substances are unknowable to us in this life. But there is surely no greater difficulty in the case of "substance" than in the case of "person." Anscombe has no right to make *selective* Wittgensteinian appeals to "ordinary language" considerations.

In "Analytical Philosophy and the Spirituality of Man" (1979),[10] Anscombe again discusses the conception of "immaterial substance." She draws on Wittgenstein's discussion of pointing in *Philosophical Investigations* §35, in which he claims that "[w]here our language suggests a body and there is none: there, we should like to say, is a *spirit*" (quoted in Anscombe, 2005, p.8). Anscombe applies this to language about the soul, or mind. As in "The Immortality of the Soul," she grants that thinking is not something material (p.9). However, talk of a "thinking (immaterial) substance" is, she suggests, an instance of "language that suggests a body," where there is none (p.10). It is really no less confused than talk of "immaterial matter" would be (p.9). She apparently presupposes that when we speak of "substances," we *must* be speaking of bodies, if we are talking sense at all. In other words, she presupposes that the *only possible* application for the term "substance" is to material things. But why should

---

[10]This paper, originally a lecture delivered at the University of Navarre in 1979, was published three years later (1982a) under the title 'On the Notion of Immaterial Substance', in O'Hara (1982).

we accept this? Here, unlike in "The Immortality of the Soul," she says nothing at all about the grammar of the term "substance," whether in its "ordinary language" or in its technical-philosophical use. It is hard not to suspect that she simply *assumes*, in "Analytical Philosophy and the Spirituality of Man" that we know no application for such expressions as "immaterial object" and "immaterial entity."

As already noted, there is indeed a difficulty in explaining how we can give sense to the idea of an immaterial entity. Furthermore, we do seem compelled to use physical imagery when talking or thinking about immaterial entities.[11] In *this* sense, it is certainly true that talk of an immaterial substance "suggests a body." But it does not follow that such talk is (virtually) self-contradictory and nonsensical. In light of her own willingness to countenance talk of "persons without bodies" in "The Immortality of the Soul," we may reasonably doubt whether Anscombe is entitled to assume that "immaterial substance" has no meaningful application. Certainly she does not argue for this assumption in "Analytical Philosophy and the Spirituality of Man." She rather takes the senselessness of "immaterial substance" for granted and offers an account, inspired by Wittgenstein, of why we nonetheless imagine that the expression is meaningful. Those who share her assumption may find this account persuasive, but the account does not justify the assumption.

I conclude that Anscombe gives no compelling reason to regard the conception of immaterial substance as "empty of content."

---

[11]St. Thomas would unabashedly admit this, since he follows Aristotle in claiming that, in this life, there can be no thinking without an image or 'phantasm'. 'Incorporeal things, of which there are no phantasms, are known to us by comparison with sensible bodies of which there are phantasms.' *Summa Theologica* Ia, Q.84, Art.7, Rep. Obj.3; Thomas (1981), p.430. (Ironically enough, in 'Analytical Philosophy and the Spirituality of Man' Anscombe *denies* that thinking always requires an image. Anscombe (2005), p.15.)

(2) *There is a way of accepting "the existence of the souls of the dead between death and the resurrection" while rejecting "temporal immortality of the soul.'* What does it mean, Anscombe asks in "The Immortality of the Soul," to say that one thing exists or happens *"at the same time"* as another, if there is no "mediating system" (Anscombe, 2008, p.78)? In the case of departed souls, she says, there is a "mediating system" in our praying for and to them (p.79). She imagines someone asking: "Are you saying that to say the dead exist between death and the resurrection is to say that people pray for and to them?" "[C]ertainly not," she replies. However, "to pray for and to them is to *say* that they exist and I know no other saying that they exist which has any content but that of an idle picture or of a superstitious fear or conventional reverence." She adds that "we can forget the idle picture."[12]

I am uncertain what Anscombe means by "mediating system."[13] I am also uncertain what she means when she says that to pray for and to the dead "is to *say* that they exist." The natural thing to say is that prayers for or to disembodied souls *presuppose* their existence, just as prayers to God presuppose His existence. Yet this is evidently not Anscombe's meaning.

---

[12]In *Philosophical Investigations* II, Wittgenstein says this: 'Religion teaches that the soul can exist when the body has disintegrated. Now do I understand this teaching?—Of course I understand it—I can imagine plenty of things in connection with it.' Wittgenstein (1958), p.178e. Anscombe would, I think, say that to be able to 'imagine plenty of things' in connection with the doctrine of the soul's disembodied existence is only to have an 'idle picture', which is of no use either in religion or in philosophy.

[13]She is partly concerned with the genuine problem of understanding temporal statements about immaterial entities. For Aristotle and St. Thomas, time supervenes on physical change. It therefore seems that immaterial entities cannot be 'in time'. How, then, could the disembodied soul exist 'at the same time' as something else? I lack the space to discuss this problem in the present paper. It will, I trust, be clear from my discussion above that, in describing the notion of *temporal* immortality of the soul as 'empty of content', Anscombe is not solely, or even primarily, thinking of the difficulty in making temporal statements about an immaterial entity.

To "presuppose" that disembodied souls exist would be to believe that they exist, *independently* of one's praying for or to them, while she wishes to claim that "saying" that they exist (hence, presumably, believing that they exist) is inseparable from praying for or to them.[14] Some Protestants who would be aghast at the thought of praying for or to the dead nonetheless profess to believe in the disembodied existence of souls. Anscombe seems compelled to say that they are talking nonsense, while Catholics who profess the same belief and *also* pray to the saints and pray for souls in purgatory are *not* talking nonsense. But how can these practices transmute into sense what would otherwise be nonsense?

Whatever Anscombe means in saying that to pray for and to the dead "is to *say* that they exist," there is a serious difficulty in her position. The Church teaches that those who die in original or mortal sin are damned and so beyond help. It is useless to pray to or for them. What, then, does it mean to say that they are damned? Or rather, how *does* one "say" this? Even if one holds out hope for the salvation of all (as Anscombe certainly did not),[15] the statement that some are or will be damned must at least be intelligible. Yet, if the only intelligible way of "saying" that a deceased person exists is to pray to or for him or her, and if it is senseless to pray to or for the damned, there seems no intelligible way of "saying" that any damned souls exist or will exist.[16]

---

[14]In one of the remarks eventually published in *Culture and Value*, Wittgenstein says, with specific reference to theological statements: 'Practice gives the words their sense'. Wittgenstein (1980), p.85. Anscombe's claim reads like an application of this remark to talk about departed souls.

[15]In the unpublished typescript of her 1989 McGivney lectures on sin, speaking of human beings living before the coming of Christ, she says that 'most of the just and holy will have been Jews' and that '[a]lmost all the rest of the world will have been lost'. 'Sin: the McGivney Lectures', in Anscombe (2008), p.152.

[16]Parallel considerations would seem to show that there is no intelligible way of saying that the devil or any of the other fallen angels exist.

Anscombe's brief and obscure account of "saying" that human souls exist between death and the resurrection by praying to and for them seems to me a somewhat contrived attempt to reconcile her Wittgensteinian hostility to immaterialist metaphysics with her staunch commitment to Catholic orthodoxy. Catholics impressed by the difficulties, real or alleged, in the conception of "immaterial substance" may feel compelled to accept this account, or something like it, if they are to remain faithful without being dishonest. Nonetheless, the account has little to recommend it.

I have sought to show that Anscombe's attack on the idea of "temporal immortality of the soul without the body" is ineffective and that her account of how one may reject this idea while still accepting Catholic teaching about the souls of the dead is implausible. I have moreover suggested that we see in "The Immortality of the Soul" a heroic but ultimately vain attempt to reconcile Wittgensteinianism and Catholicism.

The failure of this attempt should not surprise us. Anscombe remarks in "The Question of Linguistic Idealism" (1976) that Wittgenstein "detested natural theology" (Anscombe, 1981, p.123). In natural theology there is "attempted reasoning from the objects of the world to something outside the world," something that Wittgenstein took to be impossible. He took it to be impossible because he believed that we cannot meaningfully *speak* of anything "outside the world" – or outside our experience. From this it follows not only that natural theology is impossible, but that the very conception of immaterial substantiality *must* be "delusive." As St. Thomas would be the first to acknowledge, talk of the existence of immaterial entities (God, angels, subsistent departed souls) has no application to objects of natural experience. For this reason, Wittgenstein was inclined to regard such talk as senseless. This philosophical outlook is, to say the least, in serious tension with Catholic orthodoxy.[17]

We should not, therefore, expect Wittgenstein's influence on Anscombe's thinking about the problems of Catholic faith to be altogether salutary. In saying this I do not mean to detract from her real contribution to the Catholic intellectual tradition. I mean only to suggest that this contribution has lasting value perhaps *despite* Wittgenstein's influence, not because of it.

References

Anscombe, G. E. M. (1961). Aristotle: the search for substance. In G. E. M. Anscombe & P. T. Geach, *Three philosophers* (pp.1-64). Oxford: Blackwell.

Anscombe, G. E. M. (1976) (1981). The question of linguistic idealism. In G. E. M. Anscombe, *From Parmenides to Wittgenstein: the collected philosophical papers of G. E. M. Anscombe*, i (pp.112-133). Oxford; Blackwell and Minneapolis: University of Minnesota Press.

Anscombe, G. E. M. (1982a). On the notion of immaterial substance. In M. L. O'Hara (Ed.), *Substances and things: Aristotle's doctrine of physical substance in recent essays* (pp.252-262). Washington, DC: University Press of America.

Anscombe, G. E. M. (1982b). On private ostensive definition. In W. Leinfellner, E. Kraemer & J. Schank (Eds.), *Language and ontology: proceedings of the 6th international Wittgenstein symposium* (pp.212-217). Vienna: Hölder-Pichler-Tempsky.

Anscombe, G. E. M. (1984) (2005). Were you a zygote? In Anscombe (2005) (pp.39-44).

Anscombe, G. E. M. (1985) (2005). Has mankind one soul – an angel distributed through many bodies?. In Anscombe (2005) (pp.17-26).

---

[17]There has been a trend among some Catholic thinkers in recent decades to enlist Wittgenstein as a philosophical ally, especially in the wake of Kerr (1986). I consider this trend unhealthy.

Anscombe, G. E. M. (1990) (2005). Embryos and final causes. In Anscombe (2005) (pp.45-58).

Anscombe, G. E. M. (1990) (2008). The early embryo: theoretical doubts and practical certainties. In Anscombe (2008) (pp.214-223).

Anscombe, G. E. M. (2005). Analytical philosophy and the spirituality of man. In G. E. M. Anscombe, *Human life, action and ethics* (pp.3-16). Ed. M. Geach and L. Gormally. St Andrews Studies in Philosophy and Public Affairs; Exeter: Imprint Academic.

Anscombe, G. E. M. (2008). The immortality of the soul. In G. E. M. Anscombe, *Faith in a hard ground: essays on religion, philosophy and eethics* (pp.69-83). Ed. M. Geach and L. Gormally. St Andrews Studies in Philosophy and Public Affairs; Exeter: Imprint Academic.

Anscombe, G. E. M. (2008). Sin: the McGivney lectures. In Anscombe (2008) (pp.117-156).

Denzinger, H. (2002). *The sources of Catholic dogma*, trans. R. J. Deferrari. Fitzwilliam, NH: Loreto Publications.

Kerr, F. (1986). *Theology after Wittgenstein*. Oxford: Blackwell.

Pakaluk M. & Teh N. (2010). Review of *Faith in a Hard Ground*. *New Blackfriars, 91:1034*, 487-490.

Thomas Aquinas (1981). *Summa theologica* Ia, trans. Fathers of the English Dominican Province. Allen, Texas: Christian Classics.

Wittgenstein, L. (1958). *Philosophical investigations*, trans. G. E. M. Anscombe. Oxford: Blackwell.

Wittgenstein, L. (1980). *Culture and value*, trans. P. Winch. Ed. G. H. von Wright in collaboration with H. Nyman. Oxford: Blackwell.

Editors and Contributors

JUSTIN ANDERSON is Assistant Professor of Moral Theology at the Immaculate Conception Seminary/School of Theology, Seton Hall University.

JEREMY BELL is a philosophy graduate student at the University of Chicago.

DENNIS J. BILLY, C.Ss.R. is the John Cardinal Krol Chair of Moral Theology, St. Charles Borromeo Seminary, at the Archdiocese of Philadelphia.

JOSEPH M. BOYLE, JR. is Professor Emeritus of Philosophy at the University of Toronto.

JONATHAN BUTTACI is a philosophy graduate student at the University of Pittsburgh.

T.A. CAVANAUGH is Professor of Philosophy at the University of San Francisco.

PETER FURLONG is Lecturer in Philosophy at the University of North Carolina, Asheville.

DAVID HERSHENOV is Professor of Philosophy and Department Chair, University at Buffalo.

ROSE HERSHENOV is Adjunct Professor of Philosophy, Niagara University.

GEOFFREY KARABIN is Assistant Professor of Philosophy at Neumann University.

JOHN MIZZONI is Professor of Philosophy and Head of the Department of Arts & Humanities at Neumann University.

GERARD P. O'SULLIVAN is Provost and Vice President for Academic Affairs at Saint Peter's University.

PHILIP PEGAN is Associate Professor of Philosophy at Neumann University.

MICHAEL STARON is a philosophy graduate student at the Catholic University of America.

9781944769123